Rath & Strong's
WorkOut for
Six Sigma
Pocket Guide

How to Use GE's Powerful Tool to Prepare for,
Reenergize, Complement, or
Enhance a Six Sigma Program

Mary Federico

McGraw-Hill

New York   Chicago   San Francisco   Lisbon   London
Madrid   Mexico City   Milan   New Delhi   San Juan
Seoul   Singapore   Sydney   Toronto

The McGraw·Hill Companies

Copyright © 2005 by The McGraw-Hill Companies, Inc. All rights
reserved. Printed in Canada. Except as permitted under the United States
Copyright Act of 1976, no part of this publication may be reproduced or
distributed in any form or by any means, or stored in a database or
retrieval system, without the prior written permission of the publisher.

1 2 3 4 5 6 7 8 9 0   WBC/WBC   0 9 8 7 6 5 4

ISBN 0-07-143958-7

Editorial and production services provided by CWL Publishing
Enterprises, Inc. Madison, Wisconsin, www.cwlpub.com.

This publication is designed to provide accurate and authoritative information in regard to the subject matter covered. It is sold with the understanding that neither the author nor the publisher is engaged in render-
ing legal, accounting, or other professional service. If legal advice or
other expert assistance is required, the services of a competent professional person should be sought.

>   —*From a Declaration of Principles jointly*
>   *adopted by a Committee of the American Bar*
>   *Association and a Committee of Publishers*

McGraw-Hill books are available at special quantity discounts to use as
premiums and sales promotions, or for use in corporate training pro-
grams. For more information, please write to the Director of Special
Sales, McGraw-Hill, 2 Penn Plaza, New York, NY 10128. Or contact your
local bookstore.

 This book is printed on recycled, acid-free paper containing a
minimum of 50% recycled de-inked fiber.

CONTENTS

Foreword   viii

Introduction   xi

Part 1. WorkOut Basics: The ABCs of the WorkOut Approach   1

Chapter 1. A Bird's Eye View of the WorkOut Process   3
    Key Points About the WorkOut Process   3
    WorkOut Phases   4
    When to Use—and Not Use—WorkOut   8

Chapter 2. Planning a WorkOut Event   9
    The Plan Phase   9

Chapter 3. Conducting a WorkOut Event   15
    The Conduct Phase   15

Chapter 4. Implementing WorkOut Recommendations   19
    The Implement Phase   19

Part 2. Using WorkOut to Prepare for Six Sigma   23

Chapter 5. Are You Really Ready for Six Sigma?   25
    Need vs. Readiness   25
    Symptoms/Causes of Common Readiness Problems   27
    Six Sigma Readiness   30

Chapter 6. How to Know If WorkOut Can Help You Prepare for Six Sigma   34
    Where WorkOut Helps Improve Readiness   34
    Specific Help for *Your* Organization   36

CONTENTS

Moving Beyond Basic Readiness   37
Beware of Reinforcing a Disdain for Data   37

**Chapter 7. Steps to Using WorkOut to Get Your
            Organization Prepared**   42

Focus on Freeing up Resources   42
Identify Best Topics for First WorkOut   43
Define the Goal and Conduct the WorkOut   44
Introduce Basic Six Sigma Tools Where You Can   44
Publicize and Market Results   44

**Chapter 8. Illustration: WOW Auto Parts Uses
            WorkOut to Prepare for Six Sigma**   47

**Part 3. Using WorkOut to Reenergize
Your Six Sigma Initiative**   63

**Chapter 9. Is Your Six Sigma Initiative
            in Trouble?**   65

Signs of Trouble   65
Normal Ups and Downs vs. Trouble   67
Understanding Underlying Causes   69
Connecting Causes to Initiative Problems   71

**Chapter 10. How to Know if WorkOut Can Help
             You Reenergize Your Six Sigma Initiative**   73

How WorkOut Helps Reenergize Six Sigma Initiatives   73
Specific Help for Your Organization   75

**Chapter 11. Steps to Using WorkOut to Reenergize
             Your Six Sigma Initiative**   77

Identify the Best Topics for WorkOut   77
Define the Goal and Conduct WorkOuts   83

Test Your Progress   83

**Chapter 12. Illustration: Pillbox Pharmaceuticals
                          Uses WorkOut to Reenergize Its
                          Six Sigma Initiative**   84

**Part 4. Using WorkOut to Complement and Enhance
Your Six Sigma Initiative**   101

**Chapter 13. Steps to Using WorkOut to Complement
                          Your Six Sigma Initiative**   103
Selecting Six Sigma Projects   103
Identifying Problems That Are Suitable for Workout   104
So What Now?   106

**Chapter 14. Steps to Using WorkOut to Enhance
                          Your Six Sigma Initiative**   109
Making a Good Initiative Better   109
DMAIC Opportunities   109
WorkOut Habits   111
So What Now?   113

**Chapter 15. Illustration: Denny's Courier Service
                          Uses WorkOut to Complement and
                          Enhance Its Six Sigma Initiative**   114

Part 5. Using Six Sigma Tools During WorkOut   129

**Chapter 16. Using Tools Related to the Define
                          Phase of DMAIC**   131
SIPOC   131
VOC   133
Affinity Diagram   135

CONTENTS

    Stakeholder Management   137

**Chapter 17. Using Tools Related to the Measure
               Phase of DMAIC**   **143**
    Data Collection   143
    Prioritization Matrix   144

**Chapter 18. Using Tools Related to the Analyze
               Phase of DMAIC**   **147**
    The Five Whys   147
    Cause-and-Effect Diagram   150
    Flow Diagram   152

**Chapter 19. Using Tools Related to the Improve
               Phase of DMAIC**   **158**
    Brainstorming   158
    Twenty Questions   161
    SCAMPER   163
    FMEA   165

**Chapter 20. Tools Related to the Control
               Phase of DMAIC**   **168**
    Standardization   168
    Evaluating Results   169

**Part 6. Change Management and Facilitation Tips
for a Successful WorkOut**   **171**

**Chapter 21. Tips on Getting Buy-In and Cooperation
               at Each Phase of WorkOut**   **173**
    General Approach to Getting Buy-In and
        Cooperation   173
    Target Players/Situations for Stakeholder
        Management   174
    Stakeholder Analysis   176

Stakeholder Planning   179

Chapter 22. Tips on Facilitating the WorkOut Event   183
Facilitation   183
Role of the Facilitator in the WorkOut Phases   183
Difficult Situations   184

Conclusion   191

**Appendix A. Six Examples of "WorkOut for Six Sigma"
Topics and Goals, and Why They Work   192**
Using WorkOut to Prepare for Six Sigma   194
Using WorkOut to Reenergize Your Six Sigma
Initiative   196
Using WorkOut to Complement and Enhance Your
Six Sigma Initiative   198

Appendix B. But What About Lean Six Sigma?   198
Lean Six Sigma   200
How Does WorkOut Fit with Lean Six Sigma?   202
Preparing for a Lean Six Sigma Initiative   202
Reenergizing a Lean Six Sigma Initiative   205
Complementing and Enhancing a Lean Six Sigma
Initiative   206

FOREWORD
WorkOut: The Duct Tape of Process Improvement

One of the questions we like to ask clients is this: *Is your company using the most efficient and effective approach to making its processes more efficient and effective?*

The answer should be "yes." After all, you wouldn't want to use an inefficient approach to becoming efficient. And yet that's exactly what's happening in many organizations today. Over and over, we see the use of "turbo-charged" process improvement methods in situations that call for a much simpler approach.

This kind of improvement overkill is inefficient and ineffective. And it's also unnecessary. Why? Because a versatile and elegantly simple tool already exists.

Of course I'm talking about WorkOut.

I like to think of WorkOut as *the duct tape of process improvement*. It does so many things—and does them so well—that it should be part of every organization's improvement toolbox, right along with Six Sigma, Lean, and Lean Six Sigma.

But it's not enough just to have good tools. You need to

know how to pick the most efficient and effective one for the situation. And if you're doing (or want to do) Six Sigma, WorkOut can be the tool of choice to help in many situations. For example, you can use it to prepare your culture, get fast results for non-Six Sigma problems, free up resources, and make Six Sigma projects more inclusive.

Many companies have tried to address those kinds of issues in an ad hoc and unstructured way. The result has been lots of "reinventing the wheel" and very little organizational learning. A solution is to teach people how and where to use WorkOut, and then watch how they can make your Six Sigma initiative even better.

Even organizations with wildly successful process improvement initiatives have seen value in adding WorkOut to their toolbox. Take Johnson & Johnson, which has done a world-class job of making its processes "excellent" through the use of Six Sigma, Lean, and related improvement approaches. (Full disclosure: Rath & Strong was J&J's partner in its global rollout of Six Sigma.)

In its 2001 annual report, J&J's CEO attributed over $5 billion in savings to its Process Excellence (PE) activities. Still, J&J thought it was worthwhile to place another tool under its PE banner: WorkOut. Now J&J is seeing additional (and fast) process improvements as a result. (Is it a coincidence that J&J is widely credited with being the inventor—during WWII—of what was then called "duck tape"?)

I strongly believe that WorkOut has a place in every Six Sigma initiative. So Rath & Strong is delighted to help you along with our new *WorkOut for Six Sigma Pocket Guide*. It complements our other best-selling Six Sigma guides, and we hope you'll find it just as useful!

> Daniel L. Quinn
> President and CEO
> Rath & Strong Management Consultants
> Lexington, Massachusetts

• • •

Acknowledgments

The material in **Part 1. WorkOut Basics: The ABC's of the WorkOut Approach** is derived from *The GE Work-Out: How to Implement GE's Revolutionary Method for Busting Bureaucracy and Attacking Organizational Problems— Fast!*" by Dave Ulrich, Steve Kerr, and Ron Ashkenas (McGraw-Hill, 2002), and from training materials jointly developed by Rath & Strong and Robert H. Schaffer & Associates.

We would also like to acknowledge Ron Ashkenas, Matthew McCreight, and Patrice Murphy for their "Work-Out and Six Sigma" chapter in *Rath & Strong's Six Sigma Leadership Handbook* (Wiley, 2003).

Augie Stagliano and Renee Beaty, of Rath & Strong, contributed their ideas and considerable expertise and experience to this Pocket Guide. Thank you both!

INTRODUCTION
What Is WorkOut and What Does It Have to Do with Six Sigma?

The Short Answer

"WorkOut" is a structured method for bringing together a large group of people for 1-3 days to pursue an urgent, challenging business goal.

At its simplest, WorkOut involves *taking work out* of a bureaucratic process. It can also focus on more complex process improvement. WorkOut participants examine problems and brainstorm solutions … decision-makers accept or reject those solutions … accepted solutions are implemented quickly.

WorkOut connects with Six Sigma in three important ways:

1. It can *prepare* your organization for a Six Sigma rollout.
2. It can *reenergize* a Six Sigma initiative in trouble.
3. It can *complement* and *enhance* an ongoing Six Sigma initiative.

Yes, you read it right! We are indeed saying that *no matter where you are with Six Sigma*—getting ready to roll it out, experiencing difficulties with an existing initiative, or implementing it successfully—*WorkOut has a role to play*.

The More Thorough Answer

We haven't told you very much about WorkOut yet, so we wouldn't be surprised if you were thinking:

OK, it sounds promising, but how do I know it's not

*just hype? And how is WorkOut any different from a
simple problem solving meeting with an agenda and
lots of attendees?*

Glad you asked!

The combination of four factors makes a WorkOut event
very different from your typical problem-solving meeting:

1. **Who attends:** Participants include a cross-section of the
   organization, from senior decision-makers down to the
   front-line people who have day-to-day involvement in the
   process being targeted.
2. **Mindset of the decision-makers:** Senior decision-
   makers come to the WorkOut event with a bias toward
   accepting—rather than shooting down—the participants' recommendations.
3. **Speed and transparency of decisions:** Decisions are
   made during the WorkOut event itself, not days, months,
   or years later. Because decisions are made in full view of
   the participants, everyone knows what decisions were
   made, who made them, and on what basis.
4. **Multiple effects:** WorkOut addresses business issues,
   typically by rapidly eliminating unnecessary work. It
   addresses organizational culture issues through
   increased employee participation, quick and transparent
   decision-making, improved collaboration, and the building of leadership skills.

Now imagine applying an approach like this to a Six
Sigma initiative. You can use WorkOut to:

- *Prepare* for Six Sigma by:
  - freeing up resources.
  - getting your culture ready.
  - creating energy for change.
  - introducing Six Sigma tools in an unthreatening way.

- *Reenergize* a Six Sigma initiative in trouble by:
  - providing a new problem-solving mechanism.
  - getting some quick results.
  - reducing bureaucracy that's slowing down the project.
  - breaking down silos.
  - freeing up resources.
  - tweaking your culture.

- *Complement* and *enhance* an existing Six Sigma initiative by:
  - establishing a way to handle problems that are important to the business, but not suitable for Six Sigma techniques.
  - using WorkOut techniques within the DMAIC process.
  - creating behavioral habits that can be applied to—and improve—Six Sigma projects.

Want some proof? Take a look at General Electric's experience.

How GE Used WorkOut to Prepare for Six Sigma

GE was ready to dive right into Six Sigma. Seemed like a good idea: GE was a highly analytical organization that might be expected to embrace Six Sigma quickly and easily. Why not just do it?

Jack Welch had other ideas. He believed that GE's culture of analysis and auditing was actually getting in the way of action. The organization had become too hierarchical, siloed, and bureaucratic. The free flow of dialogue that is important in any organization, but vital in one as complex as GE, was being stifled.

Welch worried that a structured, data-driven approach such as Six Sigma would serve only to intensify these aspects of the culture. He feared that the overall situation would deteriorate rather than improve. So he looked instead for a way to first break down the hierarchies and the silos, "bust the bureaucracy," develop trust, and empower employees. He wanted to create a flexible culture that could do Six Sigma ... and do it right. For this reason, GE decided to implement WorkOut first.

The approach was successful under the most challenging of conditions. GE is a huge global organization filled with hard-hitting executives and managers. They were already coping with continuous change and were highly skeptical of this "newfangled" idea. But WorkOut worked. And it worked on a grand scale, across all corporate and business functions, and with the participation of over 300,000 employees in 13 different businesses around the world.

WorkOut itself has produced for GE a steady stream of business results worth hundreds of millions of dollars. But it did something even more important. It created the foundation for over a decade of further changes and developments—most notably, Six Sigma. On its Web site, GE declares:

WorkOut … opened our culture to ideas from everyone, everywhere, decimated the bureaucracy, and made boundaryless behavior a reflexive, natural part of our culture, thereby creating the learning environment that led to Six Sigma.

Your organization may not be as large, complex, or bureaucratic as GE was in the late 1980's. But if WorkOut can make it there, it can make it anywhere…

How to Use This Pocket Guide

See the inside front cover of this *Guide* for a flowchart that describes the general approach to using WorkOut for Six Sigma.

Each chapter is filled with tools (assessments, checklists, templates, etc.) that will help you use WorkOut to make your Six Sigma initiative more successful. "Illustrations" bring the use of the tools to life.

Welcome to the world of WorkOut for Six Sigma, and good luck!

What WorkOut Does NOT Involve
- A group of "subject matter experts" solving problems and making decisions in isolation
- Meetings held behind closed doors
- Months of deliberation on the right course of action
- Unexplained decisions
- Solutions forced on the people who now have to do the work differently
- Decisions that are never implemented

For more detailed information on how GE has used WorkOut, see *The GE Work-Out: How to Implement GE's Revolutionary Method for Busting Bureaucracy and Attacking Organizational Problems—Fast!* by Dave Ulrich, Steve Kerr, and Ron Ashkenas (McGraw-Hill, 2002).

PART 1

WORKOUT BASICS: THE ABCS OF THE WORKOUT APPROACH

Whether you need to read this section depends on how familiar you are with WorkOut. This pocket guide focuses specifically on how you can use WorkOut to prepare for, reenergize, or enhance a Six Sigma initiative. To do any of these, you'll need to know at least the basics of WorkOut.

Already familiar with the basics of WorkOut?

Then you can go directly to the Part of this *Pocket Guide* that addresses what you need to do with your Six Sigma initiative:

- **Prepare:** Part 2
- **Reenergize:** Part 3
- **Complement and Enhance:** Part 4

Need to learn/review some basic WorkOut concepts?

Then this Part (Part 1) is for you. It starts with an overview of the generic (i.e., not for Six Sigma) WorkOut process approach, then continues with chapters on each of the three main phases of WorkOut: Plan, Conduct, and Implement.

Need more information and guidance?

You can learn more about WorkOut in *The GE WorkOut: How to Implement GE's Revolutionary Method for Busting Bureaucracy and Attacking Organizational Problems—Fast!* by Dave Ulrich, Steve Kerr, Ron Ashkenas (McGraw-Hill, 2002). While the *Pocket Guide* you're reading focuses specifically on the use of WorkOut for Six Sigma, the book mentioned above addresses a broader range of applications, in greater detail.

CHAPTER 1
A Bird's Eye View of the WorkOut Process

The WorkOut Process

The picture below gives you a basic idea of the WorkOut approach.

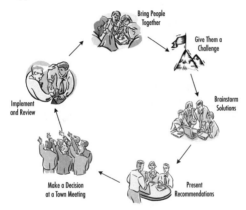

Bring People Together

Give Them a Challenge

Brainstorm Solutions

Present Recommendations

Make a Decision at a Town Meeting

Implement and Review

(Note: For general guidance on when to use—and not use—WorkOut, see **Figure 1-1** on page 8.)

Key Points About the WorkOut Process

- WorkOut brings together the *people who do the work* ... it's based on involving all levels of workers in improving the business. It provides a way for those workers to engage in a dialogue with management, (maybe for the first time!), and to jointly reach decisions.

- Each WorkOut event is designed around the *achievement of a specific goal*. This focus helps to convey the importance and rationale for change.

- Challenging people to achieve tough goals helps *break down barriers* and *eliminate the bureaucracy* that gets in the way of improved performance.

WorkOut Phases

WorkOut has three phases, each of which includes a number of sub-steps:

1. Plan the WorkOut event
2. Conduct the WorkOut event
3. Implement the WorkOut recommendations

   Tool 1a shows these phases—and their main sub-steps—on a timeline.

WorkOut Timeline

| Plan ▷ | Conduct ▷ | Implement ▷ |

Total elapsed time is typically < 120 days		
1-30 days	1-3 days	1-90 days
Before the Event	**During the WorkOut Event**	**After the Event**
• Select topic • Define goal • Organize event • Collect data • Brief key players	• Introduce WorkOut • Generate ideas • Prioritize ideas • Develop recommendations • Conduct Town Meeting	• Validate payoff • Implement plans • Track results • Review progress • Sustain results

Tool 1a.

KEY POINTS ABOUT THE PHASES OF WORKOUT

- **Importance:** While we often think of WorkOut as just the event itself, all three phases are critical to a successful outcome.
- **Duration:** The length of each phase is a function of the complexity of the problem you're working on and the availability of resources. The event itself typically ranges in length from 1-3 days.

- **Team size:** The number of participants in the WorkOut event is also a function of the complexity of the problem, and can range from 6 to 100+ people.

It sounds fairly straightforward, and it is. But at each phase there are potential mistakes that can derail the process and prevent successful outcomes. See **Tool 1b**. Don't let this happen to you!

WHEN GOOD WORKOUTS GO BAD

Mistake	Undesirable Consequences
Plan & Conduct Phases: The front line workers– those who work on the process on a day-to-day basis–aren't included in the WorkOut	• Bad data–won't know real process • Loss of good ideas from those "in the know" • Solutions that may be unworkable • Workers feel left out … likely to withhold good ideas in future

Tool 1b. (Continued on next page)

Mistake	Undesirable Consequences
Conduct Phase: The Sponsor–who has to accept or reject the recommendations of the WorkOut Teams– doesn't make a decision	• Lost opportunity for good solutions • Expectations of the WorkOut team are not met, so people unlikely to agree to participate in future improvement attempts • Wedge between management and workers
Implement Phase: Recommendations are accepted, but never implemented	• Lost opportunity for good solutions • Same issue of expectations as above, with same reluctance to participate in future improvement attempts

Tool 1b. (Continued)

More detail on the WorkOut phases, sub-steps, and participants can be found in the next three chapters in this Part of the *Pocket Guide*.

When to Use—and Not Use—WorkOut

Figure 1-1 describes the types of projects and opportunities where WorkOut will work well and those for which it is not appropriate.

When to Use WorkOut	When Not to Use WorkOut
☑ A key opportunity for improvement exists	✗ Your goal is to get buy-in for pre-conceived ideas/ solutions
☑ There is a compelling need for improved results	✗ You will not be able to implement the Team's recommendations quickly
☑ Results are needed quickly	✗ Those involved will not drive implementation
☑ Broad involvement– across functions and levels of employees–is indicated	✗ The outcome is not related to key business objectives
	✗ The outcome will be a reduction of staff

Figure 1-1.

NOTES:

Recall that in this chapter we are talking about WorkOut in the generic sense, not as it applies to Six Sigma.

See Parts 2,3, and 4 of this *Guide* for details of how to use WorkOut to prepare for, reenergize, or complement/ enhance a Six Sigma initiative.

CHAPTER 2
Planning a WorkOut Event

The Plan Phase

The purpose of the Plan phase is to put everything in place for a successful WorkOut event.

Major steps of this phase:

1. Select the topic
2. Define the WorkOut goal
3. Organize the event
4. Collect data
5. Brief key players

SELECT THE TOPIC

Most WorkOuts are focused on a specific business issue, result, or process.

The WorkOut topic should:

- address an important business objective.
- focus on performance improvement.
- include measurable goals.
- provide multiple opportunities for improvement.
- be "implementable" in no more than three months.

The planning team should prioritize potential topics by the degree to which they meet the above criteria.

See **Tool 2a** for examples of topics.

DEFINE THE WORKOUT GOAL

The WorkOut goal serves to focus the Team's efforts. It also provides a way of measuring progress/success.

A WorkOut goal should be SMART: Specific, Measurable, Achievable, Relevant, and Time-bound (or one of the many variations of this mnemonic).

Tool 2a shows examples of goals.

Depending on the size and complexity of the goal, it may be divided into smaller "team challenges." This can be done according to function, sub-process, geography, customer alignment, or some other appropriate criteria.

SAMPLE WORKOUT TOPICS AND GOALS

Topic	Goals
Improve call center customer service	Increase % of calls handled on first contact to 85% by end of March
Streamline credit application process	Decrease average turnaround time on applications from 3 days to 1 day in next 2 months
Increase Widget Department sales	Develop and introduce 2 new widget products that will generate $1M in gross revenue by end of fiscal year
Improve plant productivity	Reduce turnover rate of plant workers by 20% in 3 months

Tool 2a. (Continued on next page)

Topic	Goals
Improve customer retention	Increase customer retention for running shoe products by 10% by end of June
Increase Benefits Department productivity	Reduce department overtime costs by 50% by January 1

Tool 2a. (Continued)

ORGANIZE THE EVENT

The amount of effort involved depends on the size and length of the WorkOut. Small events can be planned in a matter of days. Bigger ones may require several weeks' lead time.

Activities at this step include:

- Create a high-level process map
- Decide on the number of teams and what they'll each be working on
- Identify participants (see below)
- Determine location/timing/dates, etc.
- Work with admin help on logistics: location, reservations, equipment, room set-up, materials, invitations, etc.

A NOTE ON PARTICIPANTS

It's important to have the right people in each of the key WorkOut roles. If you don't, the event may fizzle out.

Tool 2b provides a brief summary of the critical roles, their associated responsibilities, and some required characteristics of the people filling those roles. Information on briefing the participants appears further below.

WORKOUT CAST OF CHARACTERS

Role	Main Responsibilities	Characteristics
Sponsor (See note)	**Plan:** Approves topic and goal **Conduct:** Talks to participants about recommendations; makes decision **Implement:** Reviews progress	Supports effort Has time/interest Is biased toward accepting Team recommendations
Designer (Lead Facilitator)	**Plan:** Works with Sponsor on topic and goal; leads planning effort **Conduct:** Acts as lead facilitator **Implement:** Helps Team track results	Understands mechanics of WorkOut Has good coordination and facilitation skills
Facilitator (Secondary)	**Conduct:** Helps facilitate individual Teams; helps Designer	Has good facilitation skills

Tool 2b. (Continued on next page)

Role	Main Responsibilities	Characteristics
Team Leader	**Plan:** Briefs Team; gathers ideas and input **Conduct:** Leads Team's discussion; plans presentations **Implement:** Coordinates Team's work	Understands process or topic Has good team leadership skills
Team Member	**Conduct:** Develops recommendations **Implement:** Implements approved recommendations	Has front-line, hands-on knowledge of process or topic

Tool 2b. (Continued)

NOTE:

A Sponsor whose availability is limited may designate a Champion who will act on his/her behalf, primarily during the *Plan* and *Implement* phases of the WorkOut.

COLLECT DATA

The goal here is to provide the Teams with the basic data they'll need to come up with good recommendations. You also want to ensure that participants are dealing with facts, not just hunches. And it helps if everyone has the same set of facts at their disposal!

The WorkOut designers will determine what the Teams need to know about the process, identify what data is already available, and collect whatever else is needed. They'll put it all together into a "data pack." The pack may include cost and trend data, department reports, process performance data, process maps, etc.

Note that WorkOut is not meant to involve a lengthy data collection effort. If it will take six months to get the necessary information, it may make sense to focus first on a topic for which data is more readily available.

BRIEF KEY PLAYERS

All participants in the WorkOut should know the purpose of the WorkOut, how the event will proceed, and what will happen afterwards. They'll need details on the location, timing, what to bring, etc.

In addition to those basics, it's critical that the key players understand their roles and responsibilities. This helps ensure that the event runs smoothly, participant expectations are met, and the goal is achieved.

Sponsors should be briefed on:

- opening remarks
- Town Meeting do's and don'ts
- need for clear decisions and bias toward accepting the Teams' recommendations

Team leaders and facilitators should be briefed on:

- communicating the goal
- Team challenges
- the overall process being improved

CHAPTER 3
Conducting a WorkOut Event

The Conduct Phase

The Conduct phase is the heart of what we commonly think of as WorkOut. This is the point at which the Teams develop recommendations for reaching the WorkOut goal, and the Sponsor renders decisions.

Major steps of this phase include:

1. Introduce WorkOut
2. Generate ideas
3. Prioritize ideas
4. Develop recommendations
5. Conduct Town Meeting

INTRODUCE WORKOUT

The WorkOut event starts with a welcome and introductions. It moves on to a review of expectations, goals, the WorkOut approach, participant roles, agenda, logistics, and "house-keeping" items.

The Lead Facilitator will also introduce the Team challenges and instructions for the first work session, and distribute required or helpful materials.

GENERATE IDEAS

At the first work session, the Teams review their challenges, instructions, and relevant background information. They discuss the process to be improved, identify current problems and explore possible root causes.

Once the Teams have a shared understanding of the current state, they brainstorm ideas for reaching the goal. At this point in the WorkOut event, the goal is to generate as many ideas as possible—*not* to evaluate those ideas.

PRIORITIZE IDEAS

Once the Team has generated a sufficient number of ideas, it can begin the task of prioritizing them. This is the point at which ideas should be evaluated.

The team may develop and use a priority matrix that includes weighted criteria such as cost, practicality, timing, complexity, etc. Or it may simply categorize ideas as being *easy* or *tough* to implement and having a *big* or *small* payoff. Those ideas that are easy to implement and have a big payoff would be the top priorities. If necessary, the Team can use multi-voting to narrow the list further.

Once the Teams have finished prioritizing, it's time for the "Gallery of Ideas." At this meeting, each Team presents its top ideas to the other WorkOut Teams. The goal is to determine which ideas should be developed into recommendations; this is accomplished through multi-voting. This is also the point at which duplicate, mutually exclusive, or competing ideas are resolved and Teams realigned if necessary.

DEVELOP RECOMMENDATIONS

Teams meet to develop their top 3-5 ideas into more detailed recommendations. For each recommendation, they create a flip chart presentation that includes:

- issue

- recommendation
- payoff
- assumptions
- risks
- tracking
- action plan
- recommendation "owner"

Teams will use this "template" when presenting their ideas at the Town Meeting.

Once all the Teams are done, they do a quick run through of the presentation for the other Teams, who have a chance to provide helpful hints. This "dry run" provides a final forum for input and helps ensure broad buy-in to the ideas.

CONDUCT TOWN MEETING

The Town Meeting is the point at which the WorkOut Teams present their recommendations to the Sponsor, and the Sponsor makes an on-the-spot decision to accept or reject the idea. One of the ground rules of WorkOut is that the Sponsor should be biased toward accepting the Teams' recommendations. Another is that he/she should—if at all humanly possible—make a decision.

The Meeting begins with a welcome and a review of the process and ground rules. Teams then take turns presenting their ideas, following the template described above. The Sponsor asks questions and challenges the Team and other attendees where appropriate. He/she checks to ensure management support of the Team's recommendation, and then makes a decision.

The process is repeated for all ideas.

At the end, the facilitator recaps all decisions, explains the upcoming implementation process, and thanks the participants. The Sponsor (or Champion) makes closing remarks, and the WorkOut event ends.

CHAPTER 4
Implementing WorkOut Recommendations

The Implement Phase

In this phase, the Teams work to implement the recommendations that were approved at the Town Meeting.

Major steps of this phase include:

1. Validate payoff
2. Implement action plans
3. Track results
4. Review progress
5. Sustain results

VALIDATE PAYOFF

At the WorkOut event, the Teams used the information available to them to estimate hard and soft payoffs from their recommendations. Now it's time to validate those estimates with experts. The Teams will work with analysts to check assumptions and recalculate where necessary. They'll get agreement on what does/does not count, determine timing, and finalize the expected return.

The Teams define key measures to track the payoff—both in the short term (i.e., during the "WorkOut window" of two to three months) and long term. They will also look for leading indicators that will allow them to anticipate problems and adjust action plans quickly.

IMPLEMENT ACTION PLANS

At this step, the Teams develop and execute action plans for the approved recommendations.

Typical generic steps in the action plan include:

- collect and analyze baseline data
- test new policies, procedures, work-flows, etc.
- overcome specific obstacles
- communicate, build commitment to change
- get necessary approvals
- train, design, install, test
- hold Team meetings and review meetings with Sponsor/ Champion

Teams also develop contingency plans that will allow them to act quickly in the face of implementation obstacles.

TRACK RESULTS

Because the goal of WorkOut is to get results quickly, it typically doesn't make sense for Teams to spend time developing an automated system for tracking results. Instead, they should keep it simple. Manual checksheets or forms are fine for gathering data. What's important is that there's a *process* and a *responsible party*.

Results should be posted where those working on the process can see them. Again, this doesn't require anything sophisticated—though it helps to make charts or diagrams eye-catching. Results should be updated regularly, to reemphasize the importance of the work and to generate a feeling of accomplishment.

REVIEW PROGRESS

Each week, the Team updates the action plan to show current date, status of action steps, and progress toward payoff. Teams typically meet every week or two with the Sponsor/Champion to review progress and results and to get help with any new issues. Weekly summary progress reports are also recommended.

Additional review meetings should take place at regularly scheduled points (30, 60, 100 days) within the WorkOut period.

SUSTAIN RESULTS

It is in the organization's best interest to sustain the improvements from the WorkOut recommendations. There are several steps the Team will take to ensure this happens:

- *Capture key learnings*: Identify and document what the Teams learned about the process being improved and about the WorkOut approach itself.
- *Standardize*: Create and document job-specific instructions that are clear enough to be followed even by workers who are not fully trained.
- *Train*: Train everyone—even experienced workers—in the new process or method.
- *Develop ongoing measures*: Decide which measures to continue, and consider automating data collection for a "critical few."

PART 2

USING WORKOUT TO PREPARE FOR SIX SIGMA

You wouldn't start renovating an old house without first checking the existing structure and foundation. Why? Because it's too risky. You might spend a lot of time and money on something that later falls apart. You might have to do rework because you missed problems that are now much harder (or impossible) to fix. And you might make the mistake of tearing down things that were perfectly serviceable.

To minimize risk, you'd want to:

- Assess the state of the structure and foundation.
- Figure out what needs to be done to fix any underlying problems.
- Fix those problems before proceeding with anything more elaborate.

Likewise, it's risky to launch Six Sigma without understanding—and preparing—your organizational "foundation." You're going to be committing considerable resources and focus to this initiative. If you rush in without knowing how "ready" you are, you can delay or reduce the benefits of Six Sigma—or even miss them altogether.

This Part gives you tools to:

1. Assess your readiness for Six Sigma.
2. If you're not ready, determine whether and how WorkOut could help.
3. Use WorkOut to become better prepared for Six Sigma.

CHAPTER 5
Are You Really Ready for Six Sigma?

Want to know if your organization is ready or not? This chapter will help you assess your situation.

WHAT TO DO

- Understand the difference between *need* and *readiness* for Six Sigma.
- Refer to **Tool 5a** to help ensure you can accurately rate your organization's readiness.
- Keeping that list of symptoms in mind, use **Tool 5b** to see where you fall on the Readiness Continuum.

Note that there are many factors that go into readiness for Six Sigma. Here we've tried to hit the high points—if you don't have these, you need to do some prep work.

Need vs. Readiness

Just because you need Six Sigma, doesn't mean you're ready. You may *need* Six Sigma because:

- Measurability, predictability, and standardization are critical to the success of your business.
- You're experiencing variability in output ... You can't predict lead times, quantities, or quality.
- You're getting complaints about quality from your customers.
- You're constantly "reinventing the wheel."
- You have inspectors inspecting the work of other inspectors...

- You have errors and rework.
- Your processes are not well-defined.

You're *ready* for Six Sigma only if you have the necessary elements in place:

- leadership support, commitment, and focus
- available resources and infrastructure
- an organizational culture with at least some of the characteristics of a "Six Sigma Organization"…or the flexibility/willingness to move in that direction

Now let's see if you're ready. Start by reading through **Tool 5a**. Recognize any of these?

NOTE:

We call these "symptoms/causes" because they can be either. Some are at a deeper level than others. You should worry less about the terminology and more about identifying what's going on in *your* organization.

Symptoms/Causes of Common Readiness Problems

Lack of Leadership Commitment

❏ We seldom hear leaders talk about the need for Six Sigma.

❏ Leaders talk about the need for Six Sigma, but haven't taken any real steps to make it happen.

❏ Leaders talk about the need for Six Sigma, but their behaviors are not in line with those of a Six Sigma organization (see **Figure 5-1** on page 33 of this Guide).

Lack of Shared, Compelling Reason for Six Sigma

❏ Most of us cannot describe the consequences of *not* doing Six Sigma.

❏ We refer to Six Sigma as "the flavor of the month."

❏ We hear a lot of "It would be nice to do, but …"

Shortage of Resources

❏ We're working on multiple "high-priority" initiatives already, and can't imagine how we'd have time for more.

❏ We spend all day in meetings … the real work happens *after* work.

❏ We don't have time to plan or prevent … we just react.

Tool 5a. (Continued on next page)

HIERARCHICAL, NON-PARTICIPATIVE CULTURE

❑ We solve problems (or attempt to!) without ever involving the people who do the job every day.

❑ Front-line workers feel disenfranchised, ignored.

❑ Our quality/technical people are desperately in need of leadership and facilitation skills.

KNEE-JERK VS. DATA-DRIVEN APPROACH

❑ Leaders depend almost exclusively on their "gut" feelings, rather than data, to run their businesses.

❑ Root-cause thinking is foreign to us.

❑ We don't have any structured, rational way of solving problems; everyone does it their own way.

FOCUS ON FUNCTIONS VS. PROCESSES

❑ We have functional silos and barriers.

❑ Our processes and/or Standard Operating Procedures are ad hoc, or have evolved over years.

❑ Our reward and recognition system focuses on the performance of each individual organizational function.

CULTURE OF HEROIC EFFORTS VS. FIXING UNDERLYING PROBLEMS

❑ Fire-fighting is a way of life ... we almost encourage it.

❑ We reward short term results, even when they cause bigger problems down the road.

❑ We find ourselves fixing the same problems over and over again.

Tool 5a. (Continued on next page)

CULTURE THAT VALUES COMPETITION OVER COLLABORATION

❏ Our people optimize their own functions at the expense of the overall organization … and are rewarded for doing so.

❏ We have duplication of effort and/or things that "fall through the cracks."

❏ Nothing ever comes off our list of initiatives … nobody will let resources be reallocated away from their pet projects.

LACK OF ENERGY FOR CHANGE/BELIEF THAT NOTHING WILL CHANGE

❏ We're not ready to hear another new idea, no matter how good it is.

❏ We've been burned by previous initiatives where nothing really changed in spite of our best efforts.

❏ Nobody believes our problems will ever be fixed.

BAD EXPERIENCE OR NO EXPERIENCE WITH QUALITY INITIATIVES/ TOOLS

❏ Our past quality initiatives were poorly conceived or implemented … we have derogatory nicknames for them.

❏ Our past attempts to use quality tools were accepted by our technical people, but that's as far as it got.

❏ Our people are nervous about their ability to use quality tools effectively … see them as too complex.

Tool 5a. (Continued)

Keeping your answers in mind, use **Tool 5b** to give your organization a rating in each of the key readiness areas.

SIX SIGMA READINESS ASSESSMENT

Readiness Factors	Rating*			
	0	1	2	3
1. We have top leadership's visible and wholehearted commitment to the Six Sigma initiative.				
2. Key stakeholders (including those who will have to work differently) are clear about why we're doing Six Sigma ... and agree that it's an imperative.				
3. We have the resources to do this right: people, time, money, and attention. There are not a dozen other "key initiatives" vying for these resources.				
4. Our org culture is participative rather than hierarchical. We're willing to delegate decision making and authority to lower levels and to teams.				

Tool 5b. (Continued on next page)

	Rating*			
Readiness Factors	0	1	2	3
5. Our org culture is data-driven rather than knee-jerk. We typically solve problems and make decisions by following a rational/structured approach based on facts and root causes. We may use our intuition when appropriate, but we don't ignore the data or "shoot from the hip."				
6. Our org culture is focused on processes rather than functions. There is an emphasis on linked activities that cross functional boundaries to produce an output. We make efforts to improve these processes.				
7. Our org culture values prevention and the development of good processes over "fire-fighting." We don't reward "heroic" efforts that may solve the short-term problem but adversely affect the long-term.				

Tool 5b. (Continued on next page)

Readiness Factors	Rating*			
	0	1	2	3
8. Our org culture is internally collaborative rather than competitive. We reward collaboration between individuals, teams, departments.				
9. We have energy for more change because we've seen good results from our efforts during past initiatives.				
10. We've had good results from past quality initiatives, and quality tools are accepted and broadly used in our organization.				

*Rating: 0 = Doesn't describe us at all, 1 = Describes us somewhat, 2 = Describes us a lot, 3 = Describes us completely

Tool 5b. (Continued)

Now add up your scores from the Assessment to see where you are on the Six Sigma Readiness Continuum.

Readiness Continuum

0 – 9	10 – 16	17 – 23	24 – 30
We have a *lot* of work to do to get ready.	We've got some work to do, a few things in place.	We're close in a lot of ways, with a bit of work to do.	We're looking good!

While your overall score gives you a rough idea of how much work you've got to do, more value comes from looking at the *particular areas* in which you scored high or low.

Some readiness factors are easier to address than others. For example, it is (relatively!) simpler to find resources for an initiative than it is to change a culture that has rewarded fire-fighting into one that celebrates fixing process problems in advance. And at least one factor—past experience with quality initiatives and tools—cannot be changed at all.

But help is on the way! **Chapter 6** focuses on how WorkOut can help you address some of the more challenging readiness factors.

Finally, **Figure 5-1** lists typical behaviors of a "Six Sigma organization."

Typical Behaviors of a Six Sigma Organization
- Solves problems through
  - structured, fact-based methods that involve root-cause thinking and statistical tools
  - use of collaborative, cross-functional teams
- Incorporates the "voice of the customer" into all organizational processes
- Focuses on processes that cross functions
- Uses a common language to discuss performance
- Employs Six Sigma thinking in everyday activities, not just projects

---

Figure 5-1.

CHAPTER 6
How to Know If WorkOut Can Help You Prepare for Six Sigma

You've looked at your organization's readiness for Six Sigma, and you know you have work to do. But can WorkOut help?

WHAT TO DO

- Use **Tool 6a** to see how WorkOut can help make organizations ready for Six Sigma …
- … and to identify the specific areas where WorkOut can increase *your* organization's readiness.
- Look behind basic "readiness" and see how you can use WorkOut to be as prepared as possible (ultra-prepared!) for Six Sigma.

Where WorkOut Helps Improve Readiness

In **Chapter 5**, we gave you a tool (**Tool 5b**) to help you assess your organization's readiness for Six Sigma.

A low score on any Readiness Factor indicates that there's room for improvement in that area. But not every problem with readiness can be addressed by WorkOut.

Look over **Tool 6a** to see what WorkOut can do.

READINESS ISSUES THAT WORKOUT CAN ADDRESS

General Readiness Issue	Issue in My Org?		Can WO Help?	Comment
	Y	N		
1. Lack of top leadership commitment/support			NO	Focus first on identifying and addressing reason for lack of support
2. No shared compelling reason to do Six Sigma			NO	Focus first on creating a compelling case
3. Shortage of resources to work on Six Sigma			YES	... by getting rid of work and freeing up resources
4. Hierarchical, non-participative org culture			YES	... by pushing decisions down the hierarchy
5. Knee-jerk, non-data driven org culture			YES & NO	... by introducing basic root-cause tools. But be careful how you present the WorkOut approach.*
6. Focus is on functions, not processes			YES	... by engaging people from functions to jointly solve process problems
7. Org culture that rewards heroic, individual effort, and fire-fighting vs. prevention			YES	... by rewarding groups for solving process problems
8. Org culture that is competitive to the point of discouraging collaboration			YES	... by requiring and rewarding collaboration
9. Lack of energy for yet another change; belief that nothing will change			YES	... by engaging people in an approach that results in immediate payoff for their efforts
10. Bad experience with past quality initiatives/tools; fear or non-acceptance of tools			YES	... by introducing tools in a more effective way (also need to focus on differentiating Six Sigma from past approaches)

*See *Beware of Reinforcing a Disdain for Data!* on page 37 of this chapter.

Tool 6a.

Specific Help for *Your* Organization

Now that you have a general idea of where WorkOut can help make an organization ready for Six Sigma, identify the specific ways it can help *your* organization.

- Refer back to your scores on **Tool 5b**.
- Find the corresponding issues in **Tool 6a**. Check the Y box for areas in which you scored 0 or 1 on Tool 5b, and the N box for areas in which you scored 3. (For those in which you scored 2, make a judgment call as to whether you still need help.)
- You now have 4 "buckets" of readiness issues:
  1. Those issues that WorkOut can address, but which don't exist in your organization. You can *ignore* these.
  2. Those issues that WorkOut can address, and which exist in your organization. *You'll want to focus on these by using this Pocket Guide.*
  3. Those issues that WorkOut cannot address, and which don't exist in your organization. You can *ignore* these also.
  4. Those issues that WorkOut cannot address, but which do exist in your organization. *You'll need to address these problems*, but they are outside the scope of this *Pocket Guide*. We've provided some very quick tips on dealing with them, but you should consult a separate source for help. (Rath & Strong has written a number of books that can help.)

Chapter 7 provides further details on using WorkOut to address the issues in the second "bucket."

Moving Beyond Basic Readiness

In addition to helping you achieve basic readiness for Six Sigma, WorkOut can help you get "ultra-prepared."

An organization that's ultra-prepared for Six Sigma would be one in which people at all levels of the organization:

- Have the energy to tackle a new and complex initiative because they are confident in their ability to make meaningful changes.
- Have tangible, irrefutable evidence that senior management will involve them in making changes to their own work ... which gives them even more energy for change.

By involving employees in WorkOut events—where they are empowered to make improvements to their own work—you can create this energy and become ultra-prepared.

Beware of Reinforcing a Disdain for Data!

As you learned in Part 1, WorkOut focuses on solving process problems using the data "in the room"—i.e., what the people who work directly on the process know about how it works.

Of course we don't expect them to have performance metrics in their heads, so we collect whatever information is readily available and bring it to the room. That said, WorkOut does *not* involve the kind of sophisticated data collection and statistical analysis you find in Six Sigma.

So you may well ask:

Isn't this a problem? Why would we want to use an approach that seems to encourage fixing process problems without a lot of data? Isn't the goal to make the organization focus on using more—not less—data? Aren't we discouraging a Six Sigma mindset by introducing WorkOut? How is this good preparation for the rigors of Six Sigma?

The answer is that *it all depends on how and what you communicate*. If you can't clearly differentiate between the types of process problems that lend themselves to WorkOut, and those that require Six Sigma methods/tools, then you will indeed be giving your organization a mixed message.

Important points to emphasize:

- Using data to solve problems is an approach that will help our organization deal with the underlying reasons for its problems—not just the symptoms. This approach allows us to be more effective and efficient.

- Six Sigma provides us with the methods and tools we need to do this. It also can get us in the habit of thinking: are we looking at the real problem or just symptoms?

NOTE:

There is a fine line here. You don't want to imply that no underlying cause can be determined, and no problem solved, without complex statistics. Or that experience doesn't count for anything. This will serve only to disempower and discourage those who haven't learned the statistical methods and may never have the opportunity or ability to do so. It may also cause your most experienced people to become defensive and uncooperative—not a desirable outcome!)

- That said, not all problems require a highly analytical approach, and experience still counts for a lot. But sometimes it's hard to figure out which problems do/don't require more analysis. And it's often hard to examine our experience with a critical eye. We need to get better at this, and use the right approach for the right problem.

SEE:

- Tool 6b
- Figure 6-1

HOW TO KNOW WHEN YOU NEED MORE DATA

It's not always easy to know when you need more data and when you can just work with what you have. But here are some hints (check the ones that apply):

❏ Smart/knowledgeable people who are close to the problem:
- disagree about what's happening and why it's happening.
- feel they can't form an opinion on what's happening and why.

❏ You've tried to solve the problem based on what you think you know, but it hasn't worked.

❏ The problem has been "solved" multiple times, but always seems to recur.

Tool 6b. (Continued on next page)

❏ You've worked through the 5 Whys (see **Chapter 18**), and think you're at an underlying cause ... but this still doesn't solve the problem.

❏ The situation is one in which you have no experience.

❏ The situation has been—or still is—highly political, and there are stakeholders who have a vested interest in the status quo.

❏ There are no measurement systems in place, so it's unlikely anyone has reliable information on what's happening.

❏ The information you do have is internally inconsistent or obviously incomplete.

❏ The information you have raises more questions than it answers.

❏ Existing data collection methods rely on cooperation from people who don't necessarily want anyone to know what's actually going on.

❏ The data you have is from an unreliable system.

Tool 6b. (Continued)

Data at the Auto Repair Shop

Suppose your car is making strange and worrisome noises. Imagine two likely scenarios:

1. You have no idea what these noises are. You call your mechanic and explain the situation, but he doesn't know either. So you bring your car to the repair shop. There the mechanic runs diagnostic tests, which gener-

ate reams of data on the car's various systems. He analyzes the data, identifies potential sources of the problem, tries this and that, runs more tests, and finally fixes it. Elapsed time: 4 days. Cost: $800.

2. You think: "Hmmm, that noise sure sounds familiar." You recall an incident from two years ago, when you ran over a gizmo left in your driveway by the neighbor's kids, and it loosened your muffler pipe. Could you have done the same thing yet again? You remember seeing kids playing in the street yesterday, and vaguely recall bumping over something. So you look under the car and sure enough, the pipe is loose. You call your mechanic, and he tells you to come right in and he'll reattach the pipe.

Elapsed time: 1 hour. Cost: $30.

Sometimes you need a lot of data and complex analysis to get to the root of a problem, but sometimes you can just use what you already know...and not be any worse off. The key is to figure out which of the situations you're in, and to know what to do in each.

Generally, we use WorkOut for situations in which we (really) know what the problem is and why it's happening. We use Six Sigma methods and tools when we don't.

Figure 6-1.

CHAPTER 7
Steps to Using WorkOut to Get
Your Organization Prepared

You've identified the specific areas you need to address to become more ready for Six Sigma. And you know where WorkOut can help. Now what?

WHAT TO DO

- Focus on freeing up resources.
- Identify best topics for first WorkOuts.
- Define the goal and conduct the WorkOut events.
- Introduce basic Six Sigma tools where you can.
- Publicize and market results to create "pull."

Focus on Freeing up Resources

WorkOut got its name from its focus on *taking work out* of a process. It's difficult to imagine an organization today that couldn't benefit from this.

The beauty of using WorkOut to prepare for Six Sigma is that if you focus on freeing up resources, you will do more than address just that specific readiness factor. The WorkOuts you conduct will have side effects—and those side effects address the other readiness factors:

- Organization cultural issues:
  - hierarchical, non-participative culture
  - "knee-jerk" vs. data-driven approach (if tools introduced properly)

- focus on functions vs. processes
- emphasis on heroic fire-fighting
- competitive, non-collaborative culture
- Lack of energy for change
- Bad experience with—or fear of—quality tools

Identify Best Topics for First WorkOuts

No matter how enthused you are about WorkOut, it's unlikely that you'll be able to do it everywhere at once. You have to start somewhere … but where?

You want to ensure that you pick topics that will allow you to achieve results quickly…and get the secondary "side effects" mentioned above.

Use **Tool 7a** for hints on picking a place to start.

GUIDELINES FOR SELECTING
FIRST WORKOUT TOPICS

Look for situations with these characteristics:
- ❑ "Simple" things that seem way too complex
- ❑ Time-consuming things that are of low value
- ❑ Where there's a high level of organizational pain
- ❑ Where people agree that there's a problem
- ❑ Where an influential person thinks it's important
- ❑ Where those working on the process are complaining
- ❑ Where front-line workers have suggestions on how to improve
- ❑ Where customers are complaining, and everyone can see why

Tool 7a. (Continued on next page)

- ❏ Where the person in charge is open to new approaches
- ❏ Where there's a new person in charge
- ❏ Where important tasks are being neglected because other, less important ones are taking everyone's time
- ❏ Where there are front-line workers who have influence with peers
- ❏ Where it's somewhat obvious that there's an easier way
- ❏ Where you can get results quickly

Tool 7a. (Continued)

Define the Goal and Conduct WorkOuts

See **Part 1** of this *Pocket Guide*, Chapters 2-3.

Introduce Basic Six Sigma Tools Where You Can

See **Part 5** of this *Pocket Guide*, Chapters 17-20.

Publicize and Market Results

Done properly, a WorkOut event will allow your organization to simplify processes and free up resources. That will happen whether or not anyone else in the organization knows about it.

But to get the full benefit of WorkOut as a preparation for Six Sigma, you need to do more. If you want to affect the readiness elements related to organizational culture, you need to publicize/market the results. That way others become aware of what's happening ... and may start thinking about getting involved. See **Tool 7b.**

HOW DOES PUBLICIZING WORKOUT RESULTS PREPARE AN ORGANIZATION'S CULTURE FOR SIX SIGMA?

The WorkOut event itself models the characteristics of culture that is ready for Six Sigma.

The event involves:

- ☑ People working collaboratively across functions to improve a process.
- ☑ Employees of all levels participating in defining a problem, finding solutions, and making recommendations.
- ☑ An emphasis on fixing problems, vs. fire-fighting.

And perhaps most importantly:

- ☑ Participants are rewarded for acting this way.

The protocol of a WorkOut event requires that senior leaders make (wherever humanly possible) *on-the-spot* decisions on the participants' recommendations. It further requires that those recommendations be implemented as quickly as possible. Who wouldn't be pleased to have their efforts get those kinds of results?

New behaviors—such as collaborating, working cross-functionally, etc.—*become part of an organization's culture when people see that such behaviors lead to success.*

Tool 7b.

Some ways to publicize/market the results:

- Encourage/facilitate employee word-of-mouth to peers.
- Recognize employees involved in WorkOuts.
- Have senior leaders discuss with their peers.
- Share before and after VOC (Voice of the Customer).

CHAPTER 8
Illustration: WOW Auto Parts Uses WorkOut to Prepare for Six Sigma

Background

Augie Ramirez, recently appointed COO of WOW Auto Parts, is eager to bring Six Sigma to his new employer.

"Our competitors are eating our lunch when it comes to customer satisfaction," Augie complains to Renee Jones, WOW's VP of Operations. "And that's affecting our market share. The word on the street is that when you order a part from ABC, you never know *when* it'll show up. They say WOW stands for "When, oh when?"

Renee winces but says nothing.

"Worse," Augie goes on, "our parts aren't meeting spec. We've got to get serious about fixing our underlying problems—whatever they actually are. And Six Sigma is *exactly* the thing to help!"

Renee agrees with Augie about the need, but she's worried that WOW might not be ready to take the leap to Six Sigma.

She remembers that quality-related initiative WOW tried four years ago. Lack of leadership interest, turf wars, arguments over resources—it was *ugly*. Renee has no interest in repeating that experience. So she makes a suggestion.

"Why don't we sit down with the rest of the Operating Committee, let them know what we're thinking and do an

assessment of WOW's readiness? We should include some of
the directors also. And maybe we can get some outside help
so we know we're covering all the bases. Let's figure out
whether we've got everything we need to make Six Sigma succeed here …"

The Team Assesses WOW's Readiness

The Committee, joined by key directors and an outside Six
Sigma expert, gets together for a readiness discussion.

This group of twelve starts by looking at **Tool 5a** (see
page 27). Someone writes the list on a flip chart and they
each put a sticky dot next to every statement they feel is true
about the situation at WOW. Not everyone sees things the
same way, but at the end the ratings look like this:

WOW's RESULTS FOR SYMPTOMS/CAUSES OF COMMON READINESS PROBLEMS

LACK OF LEADERSHIP COMMITMENT	
❏ We seldom hear leaders talk about the need for Six Sigma.	••••••
❏ Leaders talk about the need for Six Sigma, but haven't taken any real steps to make it happen.	•
❏ Leaders talk about the need for Six Sigma, but their behaviors are not in line with those of a Six Sigma organization.	••

LACK OF SHARED, COMPELLING REASON FOR SIX SIGMA	
❏ Most of us cannot describe the consequences of *not* doing Six Sigma.	••••• ••••• ••
❏ We refer to Six Sigma as "the flavor of the month."	
❏ We hear a lot of "It would be nice to do, but …"	••
SHORTAGE OF RESOURCES	
❏ We're working on multiple "high-priority" initiatives already, and can't imagine how we'd have time for more.	••••• ••••• •
❏ We spend all day in meetings … the real work happens *after* work.	••••• ••
❏ We don't have time to plan or prevent … we just react.	••••• •••
HIERARCHICAL, NON-PARTICIPATIVE CULTURE	
❏ We solve problems (or attempt to!) without ever involving the people who do the job every day.	•••
❏ Front-line workers feel disenfranchised, ignored.	••••• •
❏ Our quality/technical people are desperately in need of leadership and facilitation skills.	••••

KNEE-JERK VS. DATA-DRIVEN APPROACH

❑ Leaders depend almost exclusively on their "gut" feelings, rather than data, to run their businesses.   ••••• ••

❑ Root-cause thinking is foreign to us.   ••••• •••

❑ We don't have any structured, rational way of solving problems; everyone does it their own way.   •••••

FOCUS ON FUNCTIONS VS. PROCESSES

❑ We have functional silos and barriers.   •••••
❑ Our processes and/or Standard Operating Procedures are ad hoc, or have evolved over years.   ••••• ••••• •

❑ Our reward and recognition system focuses on the performance of each individual organizational function.   ••••• •••••

CULTURE OF HEROIC EFFORTS VS. FIXING UNDERLYING PROBLEMS

❑ Fire-fighting is a way of life … we almost encourage it.   ••••• ••••

❑ We reward short-term results, even when they cause bigger problems down the road.   ••••• •

❑ We find ourselves fixing the same problems over and over again.   ••••

CULTURE THAT VALUES COMPETITION OVER COLLABORATION	
❏ Our people optimize their own functions at the expense of the overall organization … and are rewarded for doing so.	••••• ••
❏ We have duplication of effort and/or things that "fall through the cracks."	•••
❏ Nothing ever comes *off* our list of initiatives … nobody will let resources be reallocated away from their pet projects.	••••• ••
LACK OF ENERGY FOR CHANGE/BELIEF THAT NOTHING WILL CHANGE	
❏ We're not ready to hear another new idea, no matter how good it is.	••••
❏ We've been burned by previous initiatives where nothing really changed in spite of our best efforts.	••••• •••
❏ Nobody believes our problems will ever be fixed.	•••

BAD EXPERIENCE OR NO EXPERIENCE WITH QUALITY INITIATIVES/TOOLS	
❑ Our past quality initiatives were poorly conceived or implemented … we have derogatory nicknames for them.	••••• ••••
❑ Our past attempts to use quality tools were accepted by our technical people, but that's as far as it got.	••••• •
❑ Our people are nervous about their ability to use quality tools effectively … see them as too complex.	••••• ••

The group members share their perspectives on WOW's situation, then move on to do an actual readiness assessment.

They use **Tool 5b**. Here, each member assigns a rating to the different readiness factors (keeping the results of the symptom list in mind). Members share their scores, take the average for each item, and round down to get the following group result.

RESULTS OF WOW'S READINESS ASSESSMENT

Readiness Factors	Rating*			
	0	1	2	3
1. We have top leadership's visible and wholehearted commitment to the Six Sigma initiative.		✗		
2. Key stakeholders (including those who will have to work differently) are clear about why we're doing Six Sigma ... and agree that it's an imperative.		✗		
3. We have the resources to do this right: people, time, money, and attention. There are not a dozen other "key initiatives" vying for these resources.	✗			
4. Our org culture is participative rather than hierarchical. We're willing to delegate decision making and authority to lower levels and to teams.		✗		
5. Our org culture is data-driven rather than knee-jerk. We typically solve problems & make decisions by following a rational/structured approach based on facts and root causes. We may use our intuition when appropriate, but we don't ignore the data or "shoot from the hip."	✗			

Illustration: WOW Auto Parts

Readiness Factors	Rating*			
	0	1	2	3
6. Our org culture is focused on processes rather than functions. There is an emphasis on linked activities that cross functional boundaries to produce an output. We make efforts to improve these processes.	✘			
7. Our org culture values prevention and the development of good processes over "fire-fighting." We don't reward "heroic" efforts that may solve the short-term problem but adversely affect the long-term.	✘			
8. Our org culture is internally collaborative rather than competitive. We reward collaboration between individuals, teams, and departments.		✘		
9. We have energy for more change because we've seen good results from our efforts during past initiatives.		✘		
10. We've had good results from past quality initiatives, and quality tools are accepted and broadly used in our organization.	✘			

***Rating:** 0 = Doesn't describe us at all, 1 = Describes us somewhat, 2 = Describes us a lot, 3 = Describes us completely

Adding up all the 1s, 2s, and 3s, the team places WOW on the Readiness Continuum.

Readiness Continuum

x

0 – 9	10 – 16	17 – 23	24 – 30
We have a *lot* of work to do to get ready.	We've got some work to do, a few things in place.	We're close in a lot of ways, with a bit of work to do.	We're looking good!

WOW Isn't Ready—Now What?

Glum faces all around. "Well, how depressing is that?" Augie asks, not really expecting an answer. He can feel the Six Sigma initiative slipping away.

"You know, this is just an assessment, not a death sentence," Renee points out. "The idea here is not that we can't do Six Sigma. It's that we've got to do some other work first if we want Six Sigma to be a success."

This isn't having the kind of reassuring effect on the Team that Renee had hoped, so she tries again. "I mean, wouldn't you rather know about any roadblocks up front, instead of somewhere down the road after we've spent who knows how much money and we're wondering why things aren't working?"

"Yes …" Augie replies, agreeing reluctantly. "There's no arguing with your logic, but what now?"

"I can tell you 'what now'" offers Rebecca Smith, the Six Sigma expert Renee had invited to join the group. "You put together a plan to improve WOW's standing on each of the readiness factors. And if I were you, I'd consider doing WorkOut to help the situation. Are you all familiar with WorkOut?"

Nobody is, so Rebecca gives a quick explanation and describes how GE used it to prepare for Six Sigma. Augie looks skeptical. "You may not have noticed, so let me point it out: we're not GE!"

After further discussion, however, the group agrees that it might be worth a try. They turn to **Tool 6a** (see page 35) to identify where WorkOut might help.

The group agrees that, unfortunately, all 10 of the readiness issues listed in the tool are present at WOW. But they also see some good news: seven of those issues are amenable to help from WorkOut. And there are brief hints for moving forward on the others. A plan to improve readiness is within their grasp!

WOW'S RESULTS

General Readiness Issue	Issue in My Org?		Can WO Help?	Comment
	Y	N		
1. Lack of top leadership commitment/support	✔		NO	Focus 1st on identifying and addressing reason for lack of support
2. No shared compelling reason to do Six Sigma	✔		NO	Focus first on creating a compelling case
3. Shortage of resources to work on Six Sigma	✔		YES	... by getting rid of work and freeing up resources
4. Hierarchical, non-participative org culture	✔		YES	... by pushing decisions down the hierarchy
5. Knee-jerk, non-data driven org culture	✔		YES & NO	... by introducing basic root-cause tools. But be careful how you present the WorkOut approach.*
6. Focus is on functions, not processes	✔		YES	... by engaging people from functions to jointly solve process problems
7. Org culture that rewards heroic, individual effort, and fire-fighting vs. prevention	✔		YES	... by rewarding groups for solving process problems
8. Org culture that is competitive to the point of discouraging collaboration	✔		YES	... by requiring and rewarding collaboration
9. Lack of energy for yet another change; belief that nothing will change	✔		YES	... by engaging people in an approach that results in immediate payoff for their efforts
10. Bad experience with past quality initiatives/ tools; fear or non-acceptance of tools	✔		YES	... by introducing tools in a more effective way (also need to focus on differentiating Six Sigma from past approaches)

The Team Identifies Some Actions

WOW outlines a plan to improve readiness:

- Focus on getting leadership support.
- Create a compelling case for Six Sigma.
- Differentiate Six Sigma from previous quality initiatives.
- Differentiate situations that require data from those that do not.
- Initiate WorkOut events that address resource shortages and allow for the introduction of simple quality tools to a broad group of workers.

But exactly where should WOW start the WorkOut events?

Renee has a suggestion: "We've got a problem in the plant with order tracking. We've got plenty of people on it, but it's still not working well. I wonder if that's an appropriate Work-Out topic? We sure could use the resources for other things."

The Team looks at **Tool 7a** (see page 43). After some discussion of the situation, they see that the order tracking process has many of the characteristics of an appropriate WorkOut topic:

- It should be simple, but somehow it's not.
- It's not a revenue-producing process, but lots of people are working on it (with little success!).
- Both workers and customers complain about how badly it performs.
- Front-line workers seem to know exactly what the problems are, and have made suggestions.
- The managers in charge have tried everything and want

nothing more than to solve this problem.

- The plant is falling behind on a much-needed equipment upgrade because of the focus on this issue.
- The CFO has talked about the problem at the last three Operating Committee meetings.

WOW's Results for Selecting First WorkOut Topics

Look for situations with these characteristics:

☑ Simple things that seem way too complex

☑ Time-consuming things that are of low value

☐ Where there's a high level of organizational pain

☐ Where people agree that there's a problem

☑ Where an influential person thinks it's important

☑ Where those working on the process are complaining

☑ Where front-line workers have suggestions on how to improve

☑ Where customers are complaining, and everyone can see why

☑ Where the person in charge is open to new approaches

☐ Where there's a new person in charge

☑ Where important tasks are being neglected because other, less important ones are taking everyone's time

(Continued on next page)

☐ Where there are front-line workers who have influence
   with peers

☑ Where it's somewhat obvious that there's an easier way

☑ Where you can get results quickly

WOW's Results (Continued)

Looking at the list, Augie says he's starting to feel more
confident that WOW will be able to implement Six Sigma.
"OK, so we're not ready right this second. But now I see a
path. We need to flesh out our basic ideas. And with
Rebecca's help, we can get cracking on the WorkOut events
right away."

Renee nods. "And maybe—just maybe—we could get
our front-line folks to start using some quality tools. Nothing
fancy, nothing involving statistics … just the basic stuff. It
would be a great introduction to the kind of root-cause
thinking that's in dangerously short supply around here."

Augie breaks in: "And if we solve that order-tracking
problem, that would be a big load off our people. I can see
how it would start to make them feel like things might actually change for the better …"

"Yes," Rebecca points out, "but only if they don't keel over
dead first from the shock of being asked their opinions!"

SIX MONTHS LATER, AT AN OPERATING COMMITTEE MEETING …
Renee brings the meeting back to order. "OK, I've asked

Augie to give us an update on the selection of a consulting firm to help us with our new Six Sigma initiative. Augie?"

Augie jumps up. "Well, we've narrowed it down to two firms, and they'll be here to make their formal presentations next week. So we're really making progress!

"But before I go into detail on the two firms, I just want to share some feedback I got from the one out west. They asked a lot of questions about how ready we are, and I showed them the readiness assessment work we did earlier this year. When I explained how we've been using WorkOut to prepare for Six Sigma, they were really impressed—so impressed that they started taking notes!"

The group laughs, and Renee adds "Yes, thanks to WorkOut, we're a lot more ready for Six Sigma. Now we just need to make sure we roll it out right …"

PART 3

USING WORKOUT TO REENERGIZE YOUR SIX SIGMA INITIATIVE

Your Six Sigma initiative is well underway, but you're not sure it's going quite as well as it could ... and must! You've put way too much time, effort, and money into this initiative to have it fail.

Before it's too late ... before you lose the organization's attention and your funding, (and maybe your sanity!), you need to do *something*.

This Part gives you tools to:

1. Assess the state of your Six Sigma initiative—is it in trouble?
2. If the initiative *is* in trouble, determine whether and how WorkOut could help.
3. Use WorkOut to reenergize your Six Sigma initiative.

CHAPTER 9
Is Your Six Sigma Initiative in Trouble?

How do you know if your Six Sigma initiative is in trouble? How do you know if you should worry and take corrective action … or just ride out the storm? How can you make sure that if corrective action is needed, it's directed toward the cause and not the symptoms?

WHAT TO DO

- Use **Tool 9a** to see if any of these describe your initiative.
- Understand the difference between normal ups and downs and more serious trouble.
- Use **Tool 9b** to identify possible reasons for the problems you're seeing.

Signs of Trouble

Tool 9a identifies typical problems that organizations encounter in the course of deploying Six Sigma.

Look at the examples provided. Do any of these sound familiar? Are they problems your organization is experiencing? Check those that apply.

Once you've done so, move on to determine whether you're experiencing the normal ups and downs of a Six Sigma initiative, or whether something more serious is going on. If it's serious, you then need to identify (and address) the underlying cause(s) of the problem.

SIGNS OF TROUBLE IN SIX SIGMA INITIATIVES

❑ **Everything we do is a "Six Sigma project."**
Problems where the solutions are known…trivial problems … an exec's pet issue … layoffs … laptop upgrades … painting the office walls … all of these are being cast as Six Sigma projects.

❑ **Projects take *forever*, or fizzle out.**
The project can't seem to get through Define … we've been in Measure for months and still no data in sight … total elapsed time is coming up on a year and we haven't reached Control … the project is abandoned mid-way, or on hold so long nobody can remember what it was for.

❑ **Project improvements are never implemented.**
We found the root cause, figured out the right solution(s), but we never actually *implement* anything … or we implement, but things slide right back to the old way.

❑ **Project results aren't replicated.**
We've achieved some spectacular results … found some solutions that could work everywhere … but no one seems interested in capitalizing on all that was learned … so we continue to deal with the same problems, or reinvent the wheel.

Tool 9a. (Continued on next page)

❏ **We can't quantify or get agreement on results.**
We've finished our projects, but we're unable to quantify the results … or we can't get agreement on what they're worth.

❏ **Nobody wants to be a Black Belt.**
There's plenty of work to do, but we can't get people to join the BB ranks … classes aren't filling up … existing BBs ask to be released from the job prematurely … we're losing BBs to other companies.

❏ **Nobody wants to give up resources to be BBs … or Team members.**
People want to be BBs, but their departments won't let them go … we hear complaints of "you're always asking for my best people—who's going to stay here and do the real work?" … can't get people to work on the projects as Team members, even part time.

❏ **Nobody wants to Champion a project.**
We've got BBs and we have projects, but we don't have Champions … or we have Champions, but they don't do anything, and projects are hitting roadblocks as a result.

Tool 9a. (Continued)

Normal Ups and Downs vs. Trouble

The difference between normal ups and downs and trouble that needs to be quickly addressed is a matter of these four characteristics of the problems you're encountering with your initiative:

      1. Timing   3. Variety

      2. Breadth   4. Intensity

TIMING

Are the problems happening at the beginning of your Six Sigma initiative, when you would expect to stumble as you get your "sea legs"? Or are they happening after you thought you had all your ducks in a row? *Having problems after you thought things were well on track points to a more serious situation.*

BREADTH

Are the problems confined to a type of project, a department, a Champion or BB, a geographic area? Or are they widespread, without an apparent common thread? *Having widespread problems points to a more serious situation.*

VARIETY

Do the problems seem to fit into one particular type (e.g., we don't replicate solutions), or are we having lots of problems of different types? *Having a wide variety of problems points to a more serious situation.*

INTENSITY

Do the problems seem minor (e.g., we lost a few BBs, we've got a few projects that shouldn't be Six Sigma projects)? Or are they more intense (e.g., we have 50% turnover of BBs every year, most of our projects are not Six Sigma projects)? *Greater intensity points to a more serious situation.*

Understanding Underlying Causes

Why are these problems happening in your initiative? **Tool 9b** identifies some of the typical reasons. You'll need to do some further investigating to figure out which reason applies in your organization, and exactly how it applies. But this tool should get you thinking …

A word on underlying causes: We have stayed away from calling these "root" causes because we are not necessarily at that deep a level in all cases. For some of these, we've gone down a level or two. You can always use the "5 Whys" to go even deeper. A quick example:

PROBLEM: NOBODY WANTS TO BE A BLACK BELT!

> *Why?* Because they remember the XYZ initiative, where people took on special roles and were promised promotions…but never got them.
>
> *Why?* Because that deployment team didn't have a plan for following through on its promise.
>
> *Why?* Because the team spent all its time dealing with other problems.
>
> *Why?* Because the team was understaffed.
>
> *Why?* Because that initiative was just one of 25 that were going on and everyone was busy …

If this were happening in your Six Sigma initiative, you would want to look at issues relating to each "why." So: ensure you're not promising promotions if you can't follow through … if you do promise promotions, have a plan … ensure the team is properly staffed … etc.

POTENTIAL UNDERLYING CAUSES

Problem with the Six Sigma Initiative	Potential Causes*
Everything we do is a 6σ project	a b c d
Projects take forever ... or fizzle out	c e f g h i j k
Improvements are never implemented	b c e f g i j l m p
Results aren't replicated	b c e f g j m n p
Can't quantify/agree on results	c h o
Nobody wants to be a BB	b c d e f g h i j k l p q r
Nobody wants to give up resources to be BBs or Team members	b c d e g h i j k l p q r
Nobody wants to Champion a project	b c d e g h i j k r

*Cause codes:

a. No other mechanism for problem solving is available
b. We reward behavior "A" while hoping for behavior "B"
c. Lack of necessary technical/business knowledge
d. Political pressure ... push to get faster results
e. Shortage of resources/time
f. Lack of team/influence skills required to get things done
g. Competing initiatives with better rewards

Tool 9b. (Continued on next page)

*Cause codes (continued):

h. Poor project selection process
i. Don't see a compelling reason to do Six Sigma
j. Lack of buy-in
k. WIIFM not clear
l. Team not empowered to do the job or make decisions
m. "Not invented here" mentality
n. Poor communication
o. Money Belt not appropriately involved
p. Poor BB selection process
q. Bad past experience for people who take on special assignments
r. Management hasn't properly defined roles

Tool 9b. (Continued)

Connecting Causes to Initiative Problems

If there are so many potential causes of the problems you're seeing, how do you figure out which one(s) apply to your Six Sigma initiative?

There is no foolproof method for figuring this out. Very often the situation is caused by a combination of problems, intertwined with complex organization dynamics. These situations don't lend themselves easily to the use of sophisticated statistical tools. (It's unlikely that you'll be able to do a design of experiments here—though don't let us stop you from trying!)

But what *can* help is to sit with your deployment team, read through the list together, and discuss the possible causes one by one:

- Does the cause have face validity?
- Do you have any evidence that would or wouldn't support its role in causing the problem?
- Is there a way to gather additional information?
- Can you test out a theory?
- Is there something you could try that would likely work if this was indeed the cause?
- Do you have any Six Sigma tools you could use to further clarify the situation?

While not perfect, this approach can help you home in on a few likely culprits and identify a place to start.

So … is your Six Sigma initiative in trouble? If it is, WorkOut might help. See **Chapter 10** for details.

CHAPTER 10
How to Know If WorkOut Can Help You Reenergize Your Six Sigma Initiative

You've looked at your organization's Six Sigma initiative, and you've decided that it seems to be in trouble. (At the very least, it's got iron-poor blood!) You even have some ideas about the potential causes of the troubles you're seeing. So you know you have work to do. Can WorkOut help?

WHAT TO DO

- Use **Tool 10a** to get a general understanding of how WorkOut can be used …
- … and to identify the specific areas where WorkOut can help *your* organization's initiative.
- Create a final list of causes you can start to address.

How WorkOut Helps Reenergize Six Sigma Initiatives

In **Chapter 9**, we gave you tools to help you determine whether your initiative was in trouble and what might be the underlying cause(s) of the problems.

Obviously not every problem with an ongoing initiative can be addressed by WorkOut.

Look over **Tool 10a** to see what types of underlying causes can typically be addressed by WorkOut. If you believe that one of these is in play in your initiative, then WorkOut might help you get back on track.

HOW WORKOUT CAN HELP A SIX SIGMA INITIATIVE IN TROUBLE

Potential Underlying Cause of Trouble in Six Sigma Intiative	Issue in My Org?		Can WO Help?	Comment
	Y	N		
a. No other mechanism for problem solving is available			YES	... by providing an alternative mechanism
b. We reward behavior "A" while hoping for behavior "B"			NO	Focus first on educating management on this paradox
c. Lack of necessary technical / business knowledge			MAYBE	... by bringing groups together to work on a problem in detail
d. Political pressure ... push to get faster results			YES	... by getting quick results on some pressing problems
e. Shortage of resources /time			YES	... by getting rid of work and freeing up resources
f. Lack of team/influence skills required to get things done			YES	... by giving people practice in the WorkOut events
g. Competing initiatives with better rewards			MAYBE	... by getting rid of work and freeing up resources so that initiatives are not as much in competition
h. Poor project selection process			MAYBE	... by providing alternative approach for non-BB projects
i. Don't see a compelling reason to do Six Sigma			NO	Focus first on creating a compelling case
j. Lack of buy-in			MAYBE	... by showing willingness to involve key stakeholders in changing their work
k. WIIFM (What's In It For Me) not clear			MAYBE	Focus first on identifying and communicating WIIFM

Tool 10a. (Continued on next page)

Potential Underlying Cause of Trouble in Six Sigma Intiative	Issue in My Org?		Can WO Help?	Comment
	Y	N		
l. Team not empowered to do the job or make decisions			YES	... by pushing decisions down the hierarchy
m. "Not invented here" mentality			MAYBE	... by exposing people to other groups and engaging them in joint problem solving
n. Poor communication			MAYBE	... by creating new networks and "boundarylessness"
o. Money Belt not appropriately involved			NO	Get Money Belts involved at or before project selection stage
p. Poor BB selection process			NO	Focus first on creating a good competency model
q. Bad past experience for people who take on special assignments			NO	Focus first on ensuring this won't happen again, and (if possible) fixing lingering problems
r. Management hasn't properly defined roles			NO	Focus first on clarifying and communicating roles

Tool 10a. (Continued)

Specific Help for *Your* Organization

Now that you have a general idea of where WorkOut can help reenergize a initiative in trouble, identify the specific ways it can help *your* organization.

- Refer back to **Tool 10a**.
- Check "Y" for all the causes you think are contributing to your situation

- You now have four "buckets" of underlying causes:

  1. Those that WorkOut can address, but which don't exist in your organization. You can *ignore* these.

  2. Those that WorkOut can address, and which exist in your organization. These go on your list of problems to work on. *You'll want to focus on these by using this Pocket Guide.*

  3. Those problems that WorkOut cannot address, and which don't exist in your organization. You can *ignore* these also.

  4. Those problems that WorkOut cannot address, but which do exist in your organization. They belong on your problem list, but *you'll need to address these some other way*, as they are outside the scope of this *Pocket Guide*. We've provided a couple of words on how to deal with them, but you should consult a separate source (e.g., other books by Rath & Strong) for help.

Chapter 11 provides further details on using WorkOut to address the reasons in the second "bucket."

CHAPTER 11
Steps to Using WorkOut to Reenergize Your Six Sigma Initiative

You've identified the specific areas you need to address to reenergize your initiative. And you know where WorkOut can help. Now what?

WHAT TO DO

- Use **Tool 11a** to identify the best topics for your first WorkOuts.
- Define the goal and conduct the WorkOut events.
- Test your progress.

Identify the Best Topics for WorkOuts

Use **Tool 11a** as a general guideline. This tool first addresses the underlying problems with which WorkOut can *definitely* help, then continues to those with which WorkOut *may* help.

NOTE:

We are not claiming that WorkOut is the only or total solution to these underlying issues. You may need to take other corrective actions that are beyond the scope of this *Pocket Guide*.

Potential Underlying Cause of Trouble in Six Sigma Initiative	Hints for Selecting WorkOut Topics
Where WorkOut Can Definitely Help	
a. No other mechanism for problem solving is available	Look at some of your organization's problems that were inappropriately identifed as Six Sigma projects. Do they have anything in common that would suggest a topic for WorkOut? Are they the same types of (non-Six Sigma) problems? Are they in the same division? Are they all coming from a particular influential person?
	If possible, find a project that is not appropriate for Six Sigma but is being pushed that way. Solve it with WorkOut as a "proof of concept."

Tool 11a. (Continued on next page)

Potential Underlying Cause of Trouble in Six Sigma Initiative	Hints for Selecting WorkOut Topics
Where WorkOut Can Definitely Help	
d. Political pressure ... push to get faster results	If the political pressure is around solving problems that are of interest to an influential person, then you'll want to select a topic that lets you work on those problems.
	If it's general political pressure to quickly get things done, save money, free up resources, etc., then pick a topic that you think will give you the biggest win in the shortest time.
e. Shortage of resources /time	Refer to **Chapter 7**, **Tool 7a**, which focuses on freeing up resources.
f. Lack of team/ influence skills required to get things done	Almost any well-planned WorkOut can help with this issue. The key is to a) ensure the right people are involved, and b) do many WorkOuts so that they get the practice they need.

Tool 11a. (Continued on next page)

Potential Underlying Cause of Trouble in Six Sigma Initiative	Hints for Selecting WorkOut Topics
Where WorkOut Can Definitely Help	
l. Project Team not empowered to do its job or make decisions	Almost any well-planned WorkOut can help with this issue. Your goal is to show management the good that can be accomplished when a Project Team (be it Six Sigma or WorkOut) is empowered.
	The key is to find a topic in which a) the decision-maker (i.e., the person who would have to approve the WorkOut Team's recommendations) is willing to try this out, and b) you're reasonably certain that the Team would come up with workable, but not controversial, solutions. This is not the time to use WorkOut on a highly political issue!
Where WorkOut May Help	
c. Lack of necessary technical/business knowledge	Start by identifying the specific issue about which there is a lack of knowledge, and the people who need that knowledge. Then look for a topic that would allow participants to delve deeply into the issue, so that they can build the necessary technical/business knowledge as they conduct the WorkOut.

Tool 11a. (Continued on next page)

Potential Underlying Cause of Trouble in Six Sigma Initiative	Hints for Selecting WorkOut Topics
Where WorkOut May Help	
g. Competing initiatives with better rewards	Select a topic that will allow you to reduce the competition among initiatives by freeing up resources. The goal is to allow people to take on multiple initiatives instead of forcing them to choose between Six Sigma and something else.
h. Poor project selection process	Same approach as in item a, above.
j. Lack of buy-in	WorkOut is appropriate when the lack of buy-in is from employees who don't trust management to let them change their own work, and who therefore see Six Sigma as something that will be done to them without their input.
	The goal here is to select a topic that is of keen interest to this group of employees, and prove to them (by involving them in WorkOuts and implementing their recommendations) that management is willing to let them have some control of their own work. Increased trust is one of the desired outcomes.

Tool 11a. (Continued on next page)

Potential Underlying Cause of Trouble in Six Sigma Initiative	Hints for Selecting WorkOut Topics
Where WorkOut May Help	
m. "Not invented here" mentality	This mentality often stems from a need for a group (dept, team, etc.) to control its own destiny, combined with a sense that other groups don't share the same problems, goals, values, etc.
	Try to select WorkOuts that will allow key groups to come together to jointly solve problems. This can help relieve the sense of "otherness" while giving the groups even greater control of their own destiny. Increased trust is one of the desired outcomes.
n. Poor communication	Select WorkOuts that will bring together the individuals or groups who need to communicate better. Because WorkOut events involve employees of all levels, from front-line to senior management, they are an effective way of building new networks and a sense of "boundarylessness."

Tool 11a. (Continued)

NOTE:

> This Tool lists only those cases from **Tool 10a** that can, indeed, be helped by WorkOut. It does not list those for which WorkOut is not an appropriate approach.

Define the Goal and Conduct WorkOuts

See **Part 1**, **Chapters 2** and **3**, for details.

Test Your Progress

Let's not forget why you're doing this: You've determined that your Six Sigma initiative is in trouble, and you want to get it back on track.

So after you've had an opportunity to run some appropriately targeted WorkOuts, you'll want to reassess the state of your Six Sigma initiative to see if there's been any improvement. We suggest that you return to **Chapter 9**, do another assessment, and compare it to your initial one. Ask yourself:

- Do we still have any signs of trouble? Fewer, more, or no change? Same ones as before or different ones?
- Are the problems serious or part of normal ups and downs? Any improvement in the areas of timing, breadth, variety, or intensity?
- Any change in what we believe are the underlying causes for the problems? Have we eliminated or mitigated any previously suspected causes?
- Do we see progress on any objective measures of initiative success?
- Have key stakeholders started viewing the initiative as a success? What's the word on the street? (Good word-of-mouth can make people want to be involved in an initiative. And it can cause them to put more energy into making it a success.)

CHAPTER 12
Illustration: Pillbox Pharmaceuticals Uses WorkOut to Reenergize Its Six Sigma Initiativ

Background

Jean Lin, VP of Six Sigma for Pillbox Pharmaceuticals, is *not* having a good day.

First there was the call from Bob, one of the project Champions in the St Louis plant. He just told Jean that the plant manager refuses to assign anyone to the Six Sigma Team working on the tablet-coating project.

Worse, Bob reported that he had "no good counter argument" to the manager's contention that the project is ill-conceived. In fact, Bob *agrees* with the manager that the plant nee improvement results on the tablet coating process *right away* not six months from now. According to the manager, "everyon knows full well what the problem is: the process should be sir ple, but somehow it has 127 steps. And they certainly don't nee "any judo experts" to help them figure that out!

This would be bad enough by itself, but it's just the tip o the iceberg. Over the last three months, Jean has spent cou less hours listening to Champions and BBs tell her about problems with the Six Sigma initiative. The projects are taking months longer than anticipated … Black Belts don't seem to be using the DMAIC tools … improvements don't g implemented … there aren't enough project resources … and on and on and on.

Now Jean's AVP, Tim, has just dropped a new bomb on her desk. "We just had another Black Belt resign," Tim reports. "That makes nine in the last two months—three who transferred to other jobs and six who left Pillbox altogether. At the rate we're going, we'll never have a really experienced BB … someone with a dozen projects or more. They're all leaving after their first or second project. We've become the Six Sigma training company for the pharma industry!"

He pauses, but Jean doesn't say anything. So Tim continues. "So do you think we're in trouble? I mean, I expected some problems in the beginning. But I figured by now it'd be smooth sailing. After all, we've been doing this for a year. Are we missing something?"

"Maybe," Jean replies. "Maybe we need to pause and analyze where we are and why we're here. We've got some tools that can help. Why don't we sit down with the rest of the Implementation Team tomorrow for a few hours and see if we can figure this out."

The Team Assesses the Ongoing Initiative

The six members of the Implementation Team start with **Tool 9a**. First they identify the types of problems Pillbox is having. Then they discuss the characteristics of the problems to determine how severe the situation is.

Team members share the same view of how things are going: there are problems, and they are severe. The initiative is definitely in trouble. Time for some action!

The Team Identifies Causes

Given their knowledge of Six Sigma, the Team knows that they need to go beyond the surface to figure out why they're having problems with the initiative. Using **Tool 9b**, they identify 16—16!—possible reasons.

PILLBOX'S RESULTS FOR SIGNS OF TROUBLE

☑ **Everything we do is a "Six Sigma project."**
Pillbox: Based on feedback from BBs and Champions, it seems that many of our projects aren't suitable for Six Sigma. Maybe we're overusing it.

☑ **Projects take forever, or fizzle out.**
Pillbox: We have both problems: projects take a long time, then they fizzle!

☑ **Project improvements are never implemented.**
Pillbox: We know we have a problem with implementation.

☐ **Project results aren't replicated.**
Pillbox: Not a problem ... yet. You have to implement in one place before you can replicate, and we haven't gotten that far.

☐ **We can't quantify or get agreement on results.**
Pillbox: On the memorable occasions when we do close a project, we seem to be able to quantify and agree on results.

PILLBOX'S RESULTS FOR SIGNS ... (Continued)

☑ **Nobody wants to be a Black Belt.**
Pillbox: Given the turnover we're seeing, this appears to be a problem. Or maybe they just don't want to be a BB here at Pillbox.

☑ **Nobody wants to give up resources.**
Pillbox: We can't get people assigned to project teams—it's like pulling teeth. And we're starting to get pushback when we ask for resources to be BBs.

☐ **Nobody wants to Champion a project.**
Pillbox: Not a problem for us yet—but we wouldn't be surprised if it gets to this point pretty soon. The Champions are *not* happy.

PILLBOX'S RESULTS FOR SEVERITY

Severity
Characteristics of problems with the Six Sigma initiative:

Timing   ☐ At the start, as you might expect (less severe)

☑ Later when things should be going more smoothly (more severe)

*We should have been past this by now. Seems we're having more, not fewer, problems as time goes on. That **can't** be right!*

(Continued on next page)

PILLBOX'S RESULTS FOR SEVERITY (Continued)

Severity

Characteristics of problems with the Six Sigma initiative:

Breadth ☐ Confined to type of project, department, BB/ Champion, location (less severe)

         ☑ Widespread, no common thread (more severe)

> *We wish we could blame it on a few bad BBs or Champions, or some uncooperative department. But it's happening across the board.*

Variety ☐ Low: problems of 1 or 2 types (less severe)

         ☑ High: problems of many types (more severe)

> *Problems are all over the place. Of the list of eight common problems, we've got five.*

Intensity ☐ Low: a few problems, fairly minor (less severe)

         ☑ High: Lots of problems, major (more severe)

> *When we have problems, we really have them— lots of turnover, lots of projects in trouble, lots of under-resourced projects.*

PILLBOX'S RESULTS FOR UNDERLYING CAUSES

Problem with the Six Sigma Intiative	Potential Causes*
Everything we do is a 6σ project.	a b c d
Projects take forever ... or fizzle out.	c e f g h i j k
Improvements are never implemented.	b c e f g i j l m p
Results aren't replicated.	b c e f g j m n p
Can't quantify/agree on results.	c h o
Nobody wants to be a BB.	b c d e f g h i j k l p q r
Nobody want to give up resources to be BBs or Team members.	b c d e g h i j k l p q r
Nobody wants to champion a project.	b c d e g h i j k r

*Codes: *Causes associated with problems in shaded areas (above) are in bold/small caps.*

a. NO OTHER MECHANISM FOR PROBLEM SOLVING IS AVAILABLE
b. WE REWARD BEHAVIOR "A" WHILE HOPING FOR BEHAVIOR "B"
c. LACK OF NECESSARY TECHNICAL/BUSINESS KNOWLEDGE
d. POLITICAL PRESSURE ... PUSH TO GET FASTER RESULTS
e. SHORTAGE OF RESOURCES/TIME
f. LACK OF TEAM/INFLUENCE SKILLS REQUIRED TO GET THINGS DONE

(Continued on next page)

PILLBOX'S RESULTS FOR
UNDERLYING CAUSES (Continued)

g. COMPETING INITIATIVES WITH BETTER REWARDS
h. POOR PROJECT SELECTION PROCESS
i. DON'T SEE A COMPELLING REASON TO DO SIX SIGMA
j. LACK OF BUY-IN
k. WIIFM NOT CLEAR
l. TEAM NOT EMPOWERED TO DO THE JOB OR MAKE DECISIONS
m. "NOT INVENTED HERE" MENTALITY
n. POOR COMMUNICATION
o. MONEY BELT NOT APPROPRIATELY INVOLVED
p. POOR BB SELECTION PROCESS
q. BAD PAST EXPERIENCE FOR PEOPLE WHO TAKE ON SPECIAL ASSIGNMENTS
r. MANAGEMENT HASN'T PROPERLY DEFINED ROLES

The Team Sorts Through the Problems

Jean starts the dialogue. "OK, looks like we've got lots of potential underlying causes. In fact, we qualify for almost everything on the list! Maybe we can shrink this down to the ones we think are most in play at Pillbox, so we can focus on them first. Otherwise we'll just be overwhelmed."

Someone puts the list of the 16 potential underlying causes on a flip chart. The team works its way through the list, discussing each one and how it might pertain to Pillbox. There is a lot of back and forth among members.

At the end, Team members each get to "vote" five sticky dots for the causes they believe are contributing the most to Pillbox's problems.

Pillbox decides to focus on the seven underlying causes (shaded) that received three or more votes from the Team. Members agree: it's time to get this initiative reenergized!

Tim asks the question on everyone's mind: "Now, what can we actually *do*?"

PILLBOX'S NARROWED-DOWN LIST OF UNDERLYING CAUSES

a. No other mechanism for problem solving is available	•••••
b. We reward behavior "A" while hoping for behavior "B"	
c. Lack of necessary technical/business knowledge	
d. Political pressure ... push to get faster results	••••
e. Shortage of resources/time	•••••
f. Lack of team/influence skills required to get things done	•••
g. Competing initiatives with better rewards	
h. Poor project selection process	
i. Don't see a compelling reason to do Six Sigma	•••••
j. Lack of buy-in	
k. WIIFM not clear	••••
l. Team not empowered to do the job or make decisions	•••
m. "Not invented here" mentality	
n. Poor communication	
o. Money Belt not appropriately involved	
p. Poor BB selection process	•
q. Bad past experience for people who take on special assignment	
r. Management hasn't properly defined roles	

The Team Is Introduced to WorkOut

Tim takes a stab at answering his own question. "I've been reading a lot about WorkOut lately. And now that I see the issues we're dealing with, I'm thinking we could use WorkOut to help us get this Six Sigma initiative back on track."

No one else on the Team is familiar with WorkOut, so Tim gives a quick overview.

Jean likes what she's hearing. "We could make some serious progress if we had another problem-solving technique besides Six Sigma. If I could give the Champions a quicker way to deal with their process issues, they might stop pushing the Project Selection Committee to pick all these inappropriate projects. Then we could use Black Belts on the projects that really require their skills and knowledge—and maybe that would stop them from jumping ship."

Jean continued, her enthusiasm growing. "And if WorkOut can help show quick results *and* free up resources also, the department managers will be our friends forever ... and maybe they'll be more willing to give us resources for Six Sigma projects. Tim, why have you been hiding this information?"

"I wasn't hiding anything!" Tim protests. "I just didn't make the connection until we talked about the possible causes of our problems. Then it just hit me ..."

"OK, sorry! I'm just happy you brought it up," Jean replies. "Now we need to put down a basic action plan. First I guess we'll need to know which of the causes on our list could be addressed by WorkOut, and which ones are going to require some other kind of approach."

The Team Identifies Various Ways to Reenergize the Six Sigma Initiative

Using **Tool 10a**, the team is able to identify where it might be able to use WorkOut. The team looks only at the underlying reasons that made its "short list."

It's still a lot to work on. But the good news is that five of

PILLBOX'S RESULTS

Potential Underlying Cause of Trouble in Six Sigma Intiative	Issue in My Org?		Can WO Help?	Comment
	Y	N		
a. No other mechanism for problem solving is available	✔		(YES)	... by providing an alternative mechanism
d. Political pressure ... push to get faster results	✔		(YES)	... by getting quick results on some pressing problems
e. Shortage of resources /time	✔		(YES)	... by getting rid of work and freeing up resources
f. Lack of team/influence skills required to get things done	✔		(YES)	... by giving people practice in the WorkOut events
i. Don't see a compelling reason to do Six Sigma	✔		NO	Focus first on creating a compelling case
k. WIIFM (What's In It For Me) not clear	✔		NO	Focus first on identifying and communicating WIIFM
l. Team not empowered to do the job or make decisions	✔		(YES)	... by pushing decisions down the hierarchy

the underlying causes on which the Team has decided to focus are indeed amenable to help from WorkOut. And there are brief hints for moving forward on the other two. This could be the start of a plan to get the Six Sigma initiative back on track.

The Team Looks at Potential WorkOut Areas

Using **Tool 11a**, the Pillbox Team further defines the nature of the WorkOut topics that would best serve its purpose. (Again, the Team looks only at those items that both made the "short list" and can be addressed by WorkOut.)

PILLBOX'S RESULTS FOR SELECTING WORKOUT TOPICS TO ADDRESS TROUBLES WITH A SIX SIGMA INITIATIVE

Potential Underlying Cause of Trouble in Six Sigma Initiative	Hints for Selecting WorkOut Topics
Where WorkOut Can Definitely Help	
a. No other mechanism for problem solving is available	Look at some of your organization's problems that were inappropriately identified as Six Sigma projects. Do they have anything in common that would suggest a topic for WorkOut? Are they the same types of (non-Six Sigma) problems? Are they in the same division? Are they all coming from a particular influential person? If possible, find a project that is not appropriate for Six Sigma but is being pushed that way. Solve it with WorkOut as a "proof of concept."

PILLBOX'S RESULTS FOR SELECTING
WORKOUT TOPICS (Continued)

Potential Underlying Cause of Trouble in Six Sigma Initiative	Hints for Selecting WorkOut Topics
Where WorkOut Can Definitely Help	
d. Political pressure ... push to get faster results	If the political pressure is around solving problems that are of interest to an influential person, then you'll want to select a topic that lets you work on those problems. If it's general political pressure to quickly get things done, save money, free up resources, etc., then pick a topic that you think will give you the biggest win in the shortest time.
e. Shortage of resources/time	Refer to **Chapter 7**, **Tool 7a**, which focuses on freeing up resources.
f. Lack of team/ influence skills required to get things done	Almost any well-planned WorkOut can help with this issue. The key is to a) ensure the right people are involved, and b) do many WorkOuts so that they get the practice they need.

PILLBOX'S RESULTS FOR SELECTING WORKOUT TOPICS (Continued)

Potential Underlying Cause of Trouble in Six Sigma Initiative	Hints for Selecting WorkOut Topics
Where WorkOut Can Definitely Help	
1. Project Team not empowered to do its job or make decisions	Almost any well-planned WorkOut can help with this issue. Your goal is to show management the good that can be accomplished when a Project Team (be it Six Sigma or WorkOut) is empowered.
	The key is to find a topic in which a) the decision-maker (i.e., the person who would have to approve the WorkOut team's recommendations) is willing to try this out, and b) you're reasonably certain that the team would come up with workable, but not controversial, solutions. This is not the time to use WorkOut on a highly political issue!

Pillbox Outlines a Plan to Reenergize the Six Sigma Initiative

For the next hour, the Team works on putting together an initial action plan. They identify what they can do, assign tasks to the most appropriate members, and agree on due dates. The list of to-dos includes these key actions:

- Create a compelling case for Six Sigma, so that key stakeholders can understand why and where it makes sense.

- Identify and communicate the WIIFM for key stakeholders whose cooperation they need, so that key stakeholders take a personal interest in the success of Six Sigma.
  - Start immediately on a special subset of stakeholders: the BBs need to get clarity on their WIIFM while they're still around to be interviewed!

- Introduce WorkOut to the Project Selection Committee, Champions, and BBs so that everyone knows how to:
  - differentiate between Six Sigma and WorkOut projects.
  - assign the right resources.
  - use the technique to solve problems and empower employees.

- Initiate WorkOut events that will:
  - target some problems Pillbox has been trying (wrongly) to solve with Six Sigma ... especially the ones that influential leaders have been pushing to have resolved.
  - focus on freeing up resources.
  - involve the Black Belts who are having a tough time influencing others.

Illustration: Pillbox Pharmaceuticals

- – require as a decision-maker the plant manager who seems most amenable to letting employees affect their own work.

- Reassess the initiative in three months.

- Keep an ear to the ground for good word-of-mouth on the initiative, capitalize on it where possible.

After the Team disbands for the day, Jean and Tim smile at each other in relief. "Do we dare think that this could start getting better?" Jean asks.

SIX MONTHS LATER, IN AN E-MAIL TO JEAN, FROM TIM

Hi Jean,

Ready for good news? Just got off the phone with Bob from St. Louis. It wasn't a complaint—he was letting me know that the plant manager assigned five more people to the Six Sigma projects. Yeah, this is the guy who didn't want anything to do with us or our "judo experts!" What's more, Bob asked if we'd consider Sharon Evans as a BB candidate, and if we had space for three supervisors in the June Green Belt class.

I think the WorkOuts we started doing down there have really helped. Once we switched to WorkOut for that tablet-coating project, and got it fixed in three months, you could feel the change in attitude. Suddenly the PM was returning my calls. And the same thing is happening at the call center in Omaha. More on that later …

100

PART 4

USING WORKOUT TO COMPLEMENT AND ENHANCE YOUR SIX SIGMA INITIATIVE

Lucky you! Your Six Sigma initiative is up and running and things are going quite well. It's taken a lot of work to get this far, and you've experienced the usual bumps in the road. But it was worth it—your organization is getting results.

So why bother looking at yet another problem-solving approach? After all, there's a limit on how many initiatives you can reasonably deploy at the same time. And if it ain't broke …

Here's why. You can:

- *complement* your existing Six Sigma initiative by applying WorkOut to issues that Six Sigma doesn't address.
- *enhance* the effectiveness of your Six Sigma initiative by introducing WorkOut practices into DMAIC.

You can do this without an enormous amount of fanfare and commitment of resources. Read on for details ….

This Part gives you tools to:

1. Use WorkOut to help you address problems that aren't targets for Six Sigma.
2. Use WorkOut to make the steps of a Six Sigma project more effective.

CHAPTER 13
Steps to Using WorkOut to Complement Your Six Sigma Initiative

One of the most straightforward things you can do to complement your Six Sigma initiative is to *establish a mechanism for handling problems that don't warrant the use of Six Sigma methods and tools.*

Most organizations will uncover many such problems in the course of Six Sigma project selection. While it may be clear to those running the initiative that certain problems should not be assigned to Black Belts, the pressure to do so can sometimes be overwhelming. (See **Figure 13-1** page 107.)

Best bet: have an alternative approach available.

WHAT TO DO
- Use **Tool 13a** to review some of the characteristics of problems that are best suited to the Six Sigma approach.
- Use **Tool 13b** to see which of the problems not suitable for Six Sigma might be appropriate for WorkOut.

Selecting Six Sigma Projects

Tool 13a, summarizes the characteristics of problems that are suitable to the Six Sigma approach. (For detailed instructions on generating and screening project ideas, see *Rath & Strong's Six Sigma Leadership Handbook*.)

Use this checklist to screen a problem or potential project ideas. It if doesn't pass this screen, perhaps it's a candidate for the WorkOut approach.

SIX SIGMA PROJECT CRITERIA CHECKLIST

If the problem you've identified meets these criteria, it's a good candidate for a Six Sigma project:

- ❑ The problem is caused by a process.
- ❑ The process is repetitive.
- ❑ We can define a "defect."
- ❑ The problem appears opaque and/or complex.
- ❑ The solution to the problem is unknown.
- ❑ Success is measurable.
- ❑ A project to deal with this problem will have a positive effect on at least one process goal.
- ❑ There's a positive return.
- ❑ The necessary data is available.
- ❑ A project to deal with this problem can be completed in 3-6 months.

Tool 13a.

Identifying Problems that Are Suitable for WorkOut

Tool 13b lists typical characteristics of problems that might fall out of the Six Sigma screening process, but would likely be suitable for WorkOut. It also identifies characteristics of problems that are definitely *not* addressable by WorkOut.

Do any of these apply to the problems in your organization that didn't make it through the Six Sigma screen? Use the checklist to see if the problem is a candidate for WorkOut.

SCREENING PROBLEMS FOR WORKOUT

If the problem or potential project you've identified meets these criteria	
It may be a candidate for WorkOut	**It's definitely *not* a candidate for WorkOut**
❑ It requires quick resolution: 3 months or less.	❑ It involves the implementation of complex technology.
❑ You don't need a lot of data to figure out the cause of the problem.	❑ It's a highly technical situation that only a few experts can understand.
❑ You can quickly determine whether a solution works or doesn't.	❑ It requires a great deal of measurement/analysis.
❑ It involves how people (not technology systems) work.	❑ Resolution requires decisions nobody is willing or able to make.
❑ Too much bureaucracy is one of the major causes.	❑ Nobody is accountable for it.
❑ Organizational silos are getting in the way.	❑ The people responsible don't acknowledge that there's a problem.
❑ You can get the people who do the work involved in resolving the problem.	❑ Management is not willing to involve those who do the work in problem resolution.
❑ Management is willing to make a decision.	

Tool 13b.

So What Now?

Let's say you've determined that at least some of the organizational problems you're screening for Six Sigma are indeed suitable for WorkOut. What can you do to make this happen?

Here's a basic approach you can use:*

1. Have the appropriate people (you or others involved in the Six Sigma initiative) learn the WorkOut process. (See note below.)

2. Introduce the WorkOut approach to the Six Sigma project selection team so that it can be incorporated into the problem/project idea screening process.

3. Select a few appropriate problems that came out of your screening process, engage the right people, and run the first few WorkOuts. Publicize the results. (See **Tool 7a** in **Chapter 7** for tips on picking the first WorkOut topics.)

4. Provide training in WorkOut to a broader group of key people in the organization. Give them what they need to easily identify—and act on—problems that are suitable for WorkOut.

5. Use this approach yourself. No matter where you are in the organization, you can lead by example.

*Exact steps will depend on where you are in the organization, and what you, personally, can make happen.

NOTE:

We suggest that the person learning WorkOut start by observing the process, continue by assisting at an event, and then move to take a lead role in one or more of the

Plan, Conduct, and Implement phases. You may want to get outside help from someone with experience.

The goal of this approach: identify the appropriate problem-resolution approach as quickly and easily as possible, and reduce the amount of time and work the Six Sigma team must spend in screening potential projects.

Organization Dynamics in Project Selection

Applying objective criteria to potential Six Sigma projects is the easy part. What's much tougher is dealing with the dynamics that tend to surround any resource-allocation decision. Do any of the scenarios below sound familiar?

WHAT AM I GOING TO DO WITH THESE?

- Through the project selection process, you've identified problems that need resolution, but don't require Six Sigma methods/tools.
- Because you have no other mechanism for dealing with these problems, you have to either drop them or use Six Sigma inappropriately.
- If you do the latter, you'll waste resources and alienate the Black Belts, who want to work on real Six Sigma projects.
- But some of the issues are so pressing, so ripe for quick resolution, and so politically visible, that you're tempted to do it anyway.

Figure 13-1. (Continued on next page)

THE PRESSURE IS ON!
- Influential leaders are forever bringing you project ideas. When you put those ideas through the screening process, many don't qualify as Six Sigma projects.
- You've explained to the leaders lobbying for these projects why you cannot assign Belts to work on them.
- But the leaders seem uninterested in the nuances. They have problems, you have problem-solvers. So they want to know: why are you standing in the way of improvement?

HELP, WE'RE DROWNING!
- Six Sigma has been so successful that everybody and their mother wants to get on the bandwagon.
- People are coming at you with huge lists of problems they think might warrant a Black Belt, and the screening process has become unmanageable.
- You wish you could give them an alternative approach— one that they might identify as appropriate without your involvement. Then you could get back to the business of screening problems with *real* potential for Six Sigma.

So what's the solution? Have another viable way of handling the problems that don't (or won't) make it through the Six Sigma screen. And the earlier in the process you can weed out non-Six Sigma projects, the better.

Figure 13-1. (Continued)

CHAPTER 14
Steps to Using WorkOut to Enhance Your Six Sigma Initiative

Making a Good Initiative Better

No doubt you've thought of many ways to make your Six Sigma initiative better. It's likely that you've been tweaking your approach for a while. But here's something you may not have thought of: *Why not introduce WorkOut practices into the DMAIC process?*

WHAT TO DO

- Use **Tool 14a** for ideas on where you might be able to use WorkOut to enhance the effectiveness of individual Six Sigma project steps.
- Use **Tool 14b** for a list of behaviors that your Black Belts could use to good effect as they lead projects.

DMAIC Opportunities

Elsewhere in this *Pocket Guide*, (Part 5), we describe how you can use DMAIC tools in WorkOut. So it works both ways. You can apply WorkOut to Six Sigma and Six Sigma to WorkOut. *Best bet*: Don't worry about where the ideas are traditionally used. Mix and match to get the best possible results for your situation.

Take a look at **Tool 14a**. How might you take advantage of these opportunities in your initiative?

OPPORTUNITIES TO USE WORKOUT PRACTICES WITHIN DMAIC

DEFINE

❑ As you scope the project for Six Sigma, consider whether there are problems outside the scope that might lend themselves to the WorkOut approach. Pass those to a team that can initiate a WorkOut.

❑ Identify the people whose help you are going to need in order to get your project done successfully. Do any of them want help with other process issues that are not suitable for Six Sigma but that might lend themselves to the WorkOut approach? If so, providing them with help on the other problems (i.e., through WorkOut) might make it easier for them to give time, attention, and resources to your Six Sigma project.

MEASURE

❑ If you're having Gage R&R problems that involve a measuring method, (rather than a technology system or complex equipment), engage workers in a quick WorkOut to improve the method.

ANALYZE

❑ If you realize at this stage that the sophisticated statistical tools are overkill, and that the root cause is fairly obvious, recast the project as a WorkOut.

Tool 14a. (Continued on next page)

IMPROVE

❏ Once you've identified the root cause, consider whether
the situation is straightforward enough that you could
use WorkOut to identify potential improvements.

❏ Use the Town Meeting approach to get sponsor buy-in
to improvement ideas.

CONTROL

❏ If the process has been standardized, documented, etc.,
but starts to drift back, consider whether there are any
factors at play (such as bureaucracy or organizational
silos) that might be addressed through the use of
WorkOut.

Tool 14a. (Continued)

WorkOut Habits

As mentioned elsewhere in this *Pocket Guide*, WorkOut can
have a positive effect on your organization's culture. It
encourages boundaryless behavior, engages front-line workers, builds trust, reduces bureaucracy, reinforces collaboration, and so on.

But these effects don't come from theoretical discussions.
Instead, they come from people *engaging in specific behaviors, learning that those behaviors help them get work done
successfully, and then making those behaviors into habits*.

So why should this opportunity be available only to those
directly participating in a WorkOut? Shouldn't everyone—

including, for example, Black Belts—get to give these behaviors a try?

Take a look at **Tool 14b**. Wouldn't Six Sigma projects run more smoothly if everyone involved practiced acting like this? Identify the ones you could start doing *today*.

BEHAVIORAL HABITS FROM WORKOUT

Why not try these and see what happens?

APPROACH TO FRONT-LINE WORKERS

- ❏ Show respect for their knowledge and experience.
- ❏ Act on the assumption that they are interested in improving.
- ❏ Solicit—and use their ideas.

DECISION MAKING

- ❏ Be honest with others about their involvement in decisions … e.g., don't ask for ideas if you've already made up your mind.
- ❏ Strive for speed and "transparency"—let people know your assumptions and decision-making method.
- ❏ Be open to discussion about your assumptions, your methods, and your conclusion.

GENERAL INCLUSIVENESS

- ❏ Err on the side of inclusion at all stages of problem-solving.
- ❏ Look across organizational silos, at the bigger picture.
- ❏ Don't act impatient or rushed with the people you're including.

Tool 14b.

So What Now?

Let's say you've determined your organization could use
WorkOut practices and behavioral habits to enhance the Six
Sigma initiative. What can you do to make this happen?

Here's a basic approach you can use: *

1. *Have the appropriate people* (you or others involved in
   the Six Sigma initiative) learn the WorkOut process.
   (See note below.)
2. *Introduce the WorkOut approach*—and its potential
   applicability within DMAIC—to Black Belts. Encourage
   them to experiment.
3. *Use the practices and habits yourself.* No matter where
   you are in the organization, you can lead by example.
4. *Provide a support mechanism for Black Belts* who want
   to use WorkOut practices, but need some initial guidance.
5. *Include discussions of the WorkOut habits* in your
   Black Belt training and coaching, and in informal meetings. Black Belts who've used these habits to good effect
   in their projects should share their experiences and
   advice with their peer group.

*Exact steps will depend on where you are in the organization, and
what you, personally, can make happen.

NOTE:

We suggest that the person learning WorkOut start by
observing the process, continue by assisting at an event,
and then move to taking a lead role in one or more of
the Plan, Conduct, and Implement phases. You may want
to get outside help from someone with experience.

CHAPTER 15
Illustration: Denny's Courier Service Uses WorkOut to Complement and Enhance Its Six Sigma Initiative

Background

It's 1 P.M. and the Six Sigma anniversary luncheon is in full swing. But where is Jim?

Jack Woods, VP of Process Excellence, looks around the dining room but doesn't see him anywhere. "I'm sure he just stepped out for a minute" Jack reassures the directors sitting at his table. "I have to run back to my office to grab my cell phone, so I'll look around some more. I know you're all eager to talk with him."

As Jack heads back to his desk, he passes Jim's office ... and is shocked to see Jim sitting in front of his laptop, typing away.

"Jim, what are you doing here?" he asks. "The two-year anniversary of our launch is a big milestone—you should be at the luncheon, celebrating! Besides, five directors have already asked me where you are. They want to talk to you about some ideas for new projects. You're the most popular guy at Denny's since you took over the project selection sub-team!"

"I know," Jim replies, "and that's *exactly* why I'm here, instead of at the luncheon. I'm hiding! Those guys don't give me a moment's peace. It's like they've been hoarding process problems since the dawn of time, but now they want everything fixed right away—and preferably by a Black Belt."

"Hey, I think it's great that we've got their attention, and that they're comfortable asking us for help," Jack responds. "It's a sign of our success, right? C'mon, is it really *that* bad?"

"Well, I'll give you a piece of data and then you tell me how bad it is," Jim retorts.

He continues. "Of the last 150 project ideas we gathered, only a dozen were suited to the Six Sigma approach. A lousy dozen! And that's after we spent six weeks screening them. A few of the others were just trivial tasks, but most were legitimate problems that need to be fixed. Only not with Six Sigma!"

"Well, did you explain why?" Jack asks. "Maybe they just don't understand."

"Oh I explained, and they understand. They just don't want to hear it. It's in their best interest to pitch every problem as a Six Sigma project because they think that's the only way to get resources to work on it."

Jim sighs and goes on. "I'm getting a lot of pressure to just assign Black Belts and be done with it, and I have to tell you I'm sorely tempted. It'd save me a lot of time and aggravation. But I know it's not the right thing to do."

Jack nods. "Well, that much work to identify twelve projects isn't a great return—you're right about that. But you're also right about not giving in. Now I can see why you might want to hide. And I'm sure the directors at the luncheon just have more ideas for you!

"But you know," he continues, "it sounds to me like the real problem is *not* that there are too many project ideas. It's more that we don't have any alternative for the problems that don't qualify as Six Sigma projects. Right now Six Sigma is the hammer so every process problem they have is a nail! If we had something else we could give them, we wouldn't be in this situation."

"Yes," Jim agrees. "But what? Just give me something."

"I don't know," Jack admits. "But I do know who to ask: Charlene. She's back with Denny's now, and you know she's been through every iteration of process improvement known to man. I bet she's got some advice for us. She's out of town today but she'll be at our Process Excellence Management Team meeting tomorrow. We can bring it up then. Meanwhile, let's head back to the luncheon. Maybe we can hold those directors off until after we talk to Charlene!"

The Team Learns About WorkOut

Charlene does indeed have advice: use WorkOut. She describes it as "just the thing" for the implementation team—and not just for the problem Jim brought up.

"The beauty of WorkOut is that it solves multiple problems," Charlene explains. "It gives you a way to deal with process problems that don't need a Black Belt, which is your main concern right now. But you can also use some of its techniques in the course of your DMAIC projects to make *them* better. WorkOut complements and enhances a Six Sigma initiative."

Seeing that she's got their attention, Charlene continues. "The Process Excellence program at Denny's is obviously going *very* well. But this is a way to make it better—step it up a notch."

Charlene spends the next 15 minutes giving the Team an overview of the WorkOut approach. To make it more concrete, the Team decides to pick three problems from the pool of potential projects and put them through a high-level initial screening process that considers WorkOut.

The Team selects these problems:

1. On-time package delivery on Saturdays varies greatly from week to week for no discernable reason, and is a major source of customer complaints and lost revenue across the country.
2. Special payment packages are being delayed at the Omaha plant while they wait for approval, which involves multiple handoffs and signatures. The packages are consistently a day late, resulting in refunds to customers.
3. The plant in Fort Pierce has the same problem as Omaha: late packages due to a wait for approvals.

The Team Screens Problems for Six Sigma

The Team discusses the three problems in depth, sharing whatever information they have about the surrounding situation.

They conclude that all three problems meet the criteria for a Six Sigma project with the following exceptions:

- *Problem seems opaque and/or complex*: The immediate cause of Problems #2 and #3 appears to be the multiple handoffs and signatures. This is neither opaque nor complex.

- *Solution is unknown:* Again, Problems #2 and #3 appear to be solvable by a change to the approval process, so they do not meet this criterion.

(See **Denny's Results on the Six Sigma Criteria Checklist**.)

The team concludes that if it's properly scoped, Problem #1 is a likely candidate for a Six Sigma project, but problems #2 and #3 are not. If they are going to be addressed, it must be through a different approach.

DENNY'S RESULTS ON THE SIX SIGMA PROJECT CRITERIA CHECKLIST

Criteria	Prob. #1	Prob. #2	Prob. #3
Problem is caused by a process.	Yes	Yes	Yes
Process is repetitive.	Yes	Yes	Yes
We can define a defect.	Yes	Yes	Yes
Problem appears opaque and/or complex.	Yes	No	No
The solution to the problem is unknown.	Yes	No	No
Success is measurable.	Yes	Yes	Yes
A project to deal with this problem will have a positive effect on at least one process goal.	Yes	Yes	Yes
There's a positive return.	Yes	Yes	Yes
The necessary data is available.	Yes	Yes	Yes
A project to deal with this problem can be completed in 3-6 mos.	Probably	Probably	Probably

NOTE:

Shaded areas show characteristics of the problems that make them unsuitable for the Six Sigma approach.

The Team Screens Problems for WorkOut

The problems at the Omaha and Fort Pierce plants appear to be identical, so the Team wonders why it would have to bother screening both for WorkOut. Surely if one qualifies, the other will also.

Charlene cautions the Team against drawing such a conclusion without examining the problems in more detail. After further discussion, the Team concludes that the problem at the Omaha plant is a candidate for WorkOut, while the one at the Fort Pierce plant is not.

(See **Denny's' Results on Screening Problems for WorkOut.**)

Why the difference? Two reasons:

- Local management at the Fort Pierce plant has an uneasy relationship with front-line workers, and has consistently and adamantly refused to involve the workers in any improvement efforts.
- The two Fort Pierce departments involved in the approval process—Operations and Billing—have a long-standing rivalry that has adversely affected the plant's productivity for years. Local management is aware of the problem but hasn't done anything about it.

Given these conditions, it is unlikely that WorkOut—with its requirement for an inclusive approach and transparent decision-making—could succeed at Fort Pierce. In fact, the attempt might make matters worse.

DENNY'S RESULTS ON SCREENING PROBLEMS FOR WORKOUT

It may be a candidate for WorkOut		
Criteria	Omaha	Fort Pierce
Requires a quick resolution: <3 mos.	Yes	Yes
Doesn't require a lot of data to figure out cause of the problem.	Yes	Yes
Can quickly determine whether a solution works or doesn't.	Yes	Yes
Involves how people (not technology systems) work.	Yes	Yes
Too much bureaucracy is one of the major causes.	Yes	Yes
Organizational silos are getting in the way.	Yes	Yes
You can get the people who do the work involved in resolving the problem.	Yes	No
Management is willing to make a decision.	Yes	Yes

NOTE:

Shaded areas show conditions in Fort Pierce that make its problem unsuitable for WorkOut approach.

DENNY'S RESULTS FOR SCREENING PROBLEMS (Continued)

It's definitely *not* a candidate for WorkOut		
Criteria	**Omaha**	**Fort Pierce**
It involves the implementation of complex technology	No	No
It's a highly technical situation that only a few experts can understand	No	No
It requires a great deal of measurement/analysis	No	No
Resolution requires decisions nobody is willing/able to make	No	Yes
Nobody is accountable for it	No	No
The people responsible don't acknowledge there's a problem	No	??
Management is not willing to involve those who do the work in problem resolution	No	Yes

NOTE:

Shaded areas show conditions in Fort Pierce that make its problem unsuitable for the WorkOut approach.

Jack turns to Jim. "What do you think—will this help us? If we can explain the WorkOut approach to the directors and their managers, do you think they'll be willing to use it? Will it help relieve the pressure to make every problem into a Six Sigma project?"

"I think so," Jim replies, "providing we somehow teach their folks how to do it. Maybe Charlene can help us with that." Charlene nods, and Jim continues, "My only question would be: What happens to those problems that don't seem to fit the criteria for either Six Sigma *or* WorkOut, like the Fort Pierce situation? What do we do with those?"

Charlene responds, "Well there are always going to be problems that don't lend themselves to either approach. We just have to be clear about what we—the Process Excellence Group—can and can't help with."

"That makes sense to me," Jack says, nodding. "We need to keep our focus clear."

"The Fort Pierce problem seems to relate more to management's approach to managing than it does to the specific process," Charlene continues. "So that's something they have to work on, maybe with the help of someone from Organization Development. But at least we can expand our area of 'helpfulness' to include WorkOut-type problems."

Jim chimes in. "And maybe the Fort Pierce plant's management team will see Omaha solve some problems and decide they need to do it, too. I know those guys are always competing."

Charlene nods. "That could definitely happen. What we need to do is make sure word about these WorkOuts gets around. If you publicize the results, and encourage people to steal ideas shamelessly, you can get that kind of replication of projects."

"I can see that you'd have to handle that the right way, so the front-line people don't feel excluded," Jack says thoughtfully. "But if you can get one WorkOut to solve multiple problems, that's a great deal."

The Team Looks at Other Benefits of WorkOut

Jack continues, "On a related topic, Charlene, you mentioned something about also using WorkOut in our Six Sigma projects. How could we apply that here?"

Charlene replies, "Well, let's look at the list of opportunities for using WorkOut in DMAIC, and see which ones might seem appropriate for Problem #1. That was the one that involved on-time performance for Saturday deliveries. Jim, you've done a ton of projects—what do you think?"

(See **Denny's Results on Opportunities to Use WorkOut Practices Within DMAIC.**)

Jim examines the list. "Well, since we haven't started the project yet, it may be too early to know about some of these. I can't predict whether we'll have a Gage R&R problem, or whether we'll find that we don't need the Six Sigma tools to get at root causes or find potential improvements. And we're certainly going to have to scope this project down.

"That said," he continues, "I think we can definitely commit to a few of these. Certainly the ones in Define—we have the opportunity to do them with any project."

Jack picks up the idea. "Both of those suggestions address exactly the difficulties you've been telling me about, Jim. If we have another way to handle the Directors' non-Six Sigma problems, maybe they'll stop pressuring us to expand the scope or put Black Belts where they're not really needed."

"That'd be a great help to the Management Team," Jim responds. "And I know the Black Belts would sure appreciate it!"

Jack nods and continues, "And I like the Town Meeting approach in Improve. I think we should definitely start doing that where it makes sense. We can get the Black Belts familiar with these techniques at the off-site we've got coming up at the end of the month."

"We can also start talking to the Black Belts about WorkOut 'behaviors,'" Charlene adds. "There are a few of these, mostly in the areas of how you approach front-line workers, how you create a sense of inclusiveness that gets around organizational silos, and how you make decisions. Black Belts who try out these behaviors tend to make them habits after they see how helpful they are."

She continues, "And when others see the Belts acting this way—and getting results—the approach can be catching."

Jim smiles. "This is just great. I'm feeling a lot better about project selection today than I was yesterday, when I felt like I had to hide from the directors!"

Jack nods in agreement. "Me too. So let's get ourselves and some other key people trained in WorkOut. It's time to take this initiative to the next level …"

DENNY'S RESULTS ON OPPORTUNITIES TO USE WORKOUT PRACTICES WITHIN DMAIC

DEFINE

☑ As you scope the project for Six Sigma, consider whether there are problems outside the scope that might lend themselves to the WorkOut approach. Pass those to a team that can initiate a WorkOut.

☑ Identify the people whose help you are going to need in order to get your project done successfully. Do any of them want help with other process issues that are not suitable for Six Sigma but that might lend themselves to the WorkOut approach? If so, providing them with help on the other problems (i.e., through WorkOut) might make it easier for them to give time, attention, and resources to your Six Sigma project.

MEASURE

❑ If you're having Gage R&R problems that involve a measuring method, (rather than a technology system or complex equipment), engage workers in a quick WorkOut to improve the method.

ANALYZE

❏ If you realize at this stage that the sophisticated statistical tools are overkill, and that the root cause is fairly obvious, recast the project as a WorkOut.

IMPROVE

❏ Once you've identified the root cause, consider whether the situation is straightforward enough that you could use WorkOut to identify potential improvements.

☑ Use the Town Meeting approach to get sponsor buy-in to improvement ideas.

CONTROL

❏ If the process has been standardized, documented, etc., but starts to drift back, consider whether there are any factors at play (such as bureaucracy or organizational silos) that might be addressed through the use of WorkOut.

Six Months Later, in an Excerpt from Jim's Project Selection Report for April

Six Sigma: Screened 100 projects, OK'd 88 as Six Sigma, referred seven to WorkOut Team, referred four back to Directors as "just do it."

WorkOut: Trained 15 directors, faciliated 35 events.

Note: Since we introduced WorkOut, the project selection process is much more efficient. And our BBs are finally assigned to real Six Sigma projects …

PART 5

USING SIX SIGMA TOOLS DURING WORKOUT

Six Sigma Tools and WorkOut: What's the Connection?

Earlier in this *Pocket Guide*, we described WorkOut as an effective way to get your organization familiar and comfortable with some of the basic Six Sigma tools. The goal: better preparation for a Six Sigma rollout.

Done properly, WorkOut is an inclusive process that can help foster learning across all levels of an organization. It lets you introduce people to tools in a natural and non-threatening way, i.e., as they work collaboratively to improve a familiar process.

In this Section, we identify some of the common DMAIC tools that lend themselves to use during the WorkOut phases.

We've organized these tools according to the phase of DMAIC in which you'd typically use them. Although some Six Sigma tools are used in more than one phase of DMAIC, we address each tool only once.

Within each chapter, we indicate the phases of WorkOut in which you are likely to use the tools. Note that:

- tools may be appropriate in one, two or all three WorkOut phases.

- although most WorkOut participants are involved only in the Conduct and Implement phases, we also include (where appropriate) information on use of the tools in the Plan phase.

More information on these and other Six Sigma tools can be found in *Rath & Strong's Six Sigma Pocket Guide*.

CHAPTER 16
Using Tools Related to the Define Phase of DMAIC

In this Chapter, we will address WorkOut-appropriate tools that are typically used in the Define phase of the DMAIC process:

1. SIPOC
2. VOC
3. Affinity Diagram
4. Stakeholder Management

SIPOC

WHAT IT IS

A SIPOC is a high-level process map that includes:

- **S**uppliers: those providing input to the process
- **I**nputs: what the suppliers provide
- **P**rocess: what's done with the input
- **O**utputs: what comes out of the process
- **C**ustomers: who gets the output

See **Tool 16a**. You can use this template for any SIPOC.

EXAMPLE OF A *SIPOC* FOR MAKING A PHOTOCOPY

SUPPLIERS	INPUTS	PROCESS	OUTPUTS	CUSTOMERS
Mfrs.	Copier		Copies	You
Office Supply Co.	Paper	See Process Steps Below		File
	Toner			Others
You	Original			
Electric Co.	Power			

Put original on glass	→	Close lid	→	Adjust settings	→	Press START	→	Remove originals & copies

Process Steps

Tool 16a.

WHEN AND WHY IT'S USED IN WORKOUT

In the *Conduct* phase, use SIPOC:

- to create an accurate, high-level (4-7 step) picture of the process (before delving into the details).
- to ensure team members are all viewing the process in the same way.
- to show leaders what the team is working on.
- to bound the process, so that the scope of the team's problem-solving is clear and manageable.

- to identify points at which there may be the potential for streamlining or improving quality.

WHAT TO DO

Start by asking some questions about the process that will get everyone thinking:

- *Purpose:* Why does this process exist?
- *Outputs:* What products/service does it make?
- *Customers:* Who uses the product/service?
- *Inputs/Suppliers:* Where does the information or material you work on come from? Who are your suppliers? What do they supply?
- *Process Steps:* What happens to each input?

  Then:

1. Name the process.
2. Clarify process stop/start (boundaries).
3. List key outputs and customers.
4. List key inputs and suppliers.
5. Identify, name, and order the major steps.

VOC

WHAT IT IS

Voice of the Customer is used to describe customers' needs and their perceptions of your product or service. We sometimes also use the term VOC for the process we go through in order to get that information about customers.

Customers for a process can be internal (within the company) or external.

WHEN AND WHY IT'S USED IN WORKOUT

In the *Plan* phase, use VOC:

- to help determine the right WorkOut topic and goal.
- to create a rallying point for those being invited to participate in the WorkOut event.
- to get a baseline measure of customer satisfaction.

In the *Conduct* phase, use VOC:

- to highlight key problems.
- to decide where to focus improvement efforts.
- as a criteria in evaluating/prioritizing potential recommendations.

In the *Implement* phase, use VOC:

- as part of the equation for validating the payoff of the recommendations.
- to track results and review progress.

WHAT TO DO

Follow the steps shown in **Tool 16b**.

NOTE:

- *Reactive* sources include customer complaints, service calls, returns, warranty claims.
- *Proactive* sources include interviews, focus groups, surveys.
- *CTQs* are those requirements that are Critical to Quality.

THE VOC PROCESS

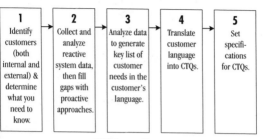

1	2	3	4	5
Identify customers (both internal and external) & determine what you need to know.	Collect and analyze reactive system data, then fill gaps with proactive approaches.	Analyze data to generate key list of customer needs in the customer's language.	Translate customer language into CTQs.	Set specifications for CTQs.

VOC Process Steps

Tool 16b.

Affinity Diagram

WHAT IT IS

An Affinity Diagram is a tool that organizes "language data" (written ideas/items) into related groups. In creating an Affinity Diagram, statements are written on individual notes, themes are identified, and notes are clustered under the themes.

The process of creating an Affinity Diagram stresses creative or intuitive thinking, with ideas clustered based on intuition, rather than hard logic.

LIST OF ITEMS BEFORE USING AFFINITY DIAGRAM

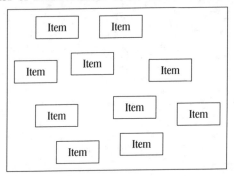

LIST OF ITEMS AFTER USING AFFINITY DIAGRAM

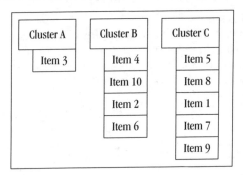

WHEN AND WHY IT'S USED IN WORKOUT

In the *Plan* phase, use Affinity Diagrams:

- to organize ideas, issues, and opinions related to the selection of WorkOut topics and goals.
- to organize VOC data.

In the *Conduct* phase, use Affinity Diagrams:

- to deal with results of brainstorming.
  to identify patterns in the participants' experience with the process.
- to organize potential improvement ideas.
- to encourage ownership of results.

WHAT TO DO

1. Write statements on individual cards or sticky notes.
2. Cluster the notes based on intuition, not logic. Do this silently. If you disagree with a note's placement, move it. If you disagree with where someone moves a note, move it back. Discuss later.
3. Give titles to each cluster of notes. The title should identify the theme of the notes.
4. Discuss the finished product with the team.

There can be several layers of clusters, and one note can be its own cluster if it's not related to any other notes.

Stakeholder Management

WHAT IT IS

Stakeholder Management is a structured approach to dealing

with the "people side" of a process change.

If you want to implement and sustain improvements, you need some degree of cooperation or buy-in from those who have a stake in the process that you're changing. The key is to identify relevant stakeholders, analyze their situation and what you need from them, and create a plan to get the necessary support.

This includes a very detailed analysis and planning approach.

- For further details on stakeholder management, refer to **Chapter 21** of this *Guide*. See *Rath & Strong's Six Sigma Team Pocket Guide* for an even more comprehensive approach.
- For a quick approach that can be useful in WorkOut, read further.

WHEN AND WHY IT'S USED IN WORKOUT

In the *Plan* phase, use Stakeholder Management:

- to identify the stakeholders of the process that is the focus of the WorkOut, so that you know whom to invite to the event.
- to anticipate—and address in advance—potential resistance from stakeholders to examining or changing the process.
- to ensure that those leaders coming to the WorkOut event are biased toward supporting the Team's recommendations.

In the *Conduct* phase, use Stakeholder Management:

- to identify others who may be affected by the Team's recommended improvements.
- to anticipate—and address in advance—potential resistance to implementing the recommendations.
- to send a signal to the Team and Leaders that the effect on people is an important consideration.

In the *Implement* phase, use Stakeholder Management:

- to ensure the right people are involved.
- to reexamine stakeholders to see if new areas of resistance have arisen now that more details of the changes are known.

WHAT TO DO

1. Use **Tool 16c** to identify stakeholders.
2. Use **Tool 16d** to create a commitment scale.
3. Determine each stakeholder's current level of commitment to the changes you're looking to make (indicate with a dot).
4. Determine the level of commitment you'll need from each stakeholder in order to successfully implement/sustain the change (indicate with an x).
5. Use the gap between current and desired levels of commitment to identify the amount of work required and to prioritize efforts.

STAKEHOLDER IDENTIFICATION CHECKLIST

Consider "obvious" stakeholders:	
❏ Sponsor ❏ Champion ❏ The owner of the process you're working on	❏ Those who work directly on the target process ❏ Members of your Project Team ❏ Your boss

Consider not-so-obvious stakeholders:	
❏ People who work indirectly on the process, or who are suppliers/customers to it ❏ Those responsible for originally designing the process ❏ Those who have been managing the process ❏ The "organizational heroes" who have been fixing past or current problems on the process	❏ Those responsible for technology systems that support the process ❏ People who are back-filling for those on the Project Team ❏ Anyone who may be perceived as incapable of solving the problem if they use outside help ❏ Anyone who could lose face if others find out that the process is performing poorly

Tool 16c. (Continued on next page)

Expand by thinking of all the major activities of your project. Then:	
❏ Identify individuals or groups who are affected by each activity	❏ Identify individuals or groups who could affect the success of each activity
Finally, look at each stakeholder you've identified and consider whether you should include:	
❏ The person's manager	❏ The person's direct reports

Tool 16c. (Continued)

STAKEHOLDER ANALYSIS COMMITMENT SCALE

Level of Commitment	People or Groups		
	Sales	Mgmt	Cust.
Enthusiastic support: Will work hard to make it happen	●		●
Help it work: Will lend appropriate support to implement the solution		●	
Compliant: Will do minimal acceptable and will try to erode the standard			
Hesitant: Holds some reservations, won't volunteer			
Indifferent: Won't help, won't hurt			X
Uncooperative: Will have to be prodded		X	
Opposed: Will openly act on and state opposition to the solution	X		
Hostile: Will block implementation of the solution at all cost			

Tool 16d.

CHAPTER 17
Using Tools Related to the Measure Phase of DMAIC

In this Chapter, we will address WorkOut-appropriate tools that are typically used in the *Measure* phase of the DMAIC process:

1. Data Collection
2. Prioritization Matrix

Data Collection

WHAT IT IS

Data Collection involves identifying and gathering the information necessary to build a factual understanding of existing process conditions and problems. That knowledge will help you narrow the range of potential improvements.

WHEN AND WHY IT'S USED IN WORKOUT

In the *Plan* phase, use Data Collection:

- to ensure that the participants will have access to available information about the process, and can use it to identify improvements.
- to ensure that senior leaders can make on-the-spot decisions instead of requests for additional data.

NOTE:

In Chapter 5 of this *Guide*, we stress that WorkOut does not involve the kind of sophisticated data collection (or analysis) you find in Six Sigma. Instead, it focuses on using the data "in the room." But it's the responsibility of the WorkOut Planning Team to ensure that *existing information about the process* is indeed available to participants in the event room.

WHAT TO DO

- Identify the process your WorkOut event will address.
- Refer to the WorkOut goal for the process. Determine what measures you will use to identify a baseline and progress toward that goal. (Your SIPOC is a good starting point.)
- Identify and pull together any currently available reports (formal and informal), files, spreadsheets, etc. that provide information on the key measures.
- Identify gaps: information you'll need that you currently do not have. Determine whether it's possible to collect this information quickly and easily. (Problems for which you do not have quick and easy access to data are probably not the best WorkOut targets.)
- Create a plan to quickly pull together the missing information in a way that makes it usable at the WorkOut event.

Prioritization Matrix

WHAT IT IS

A prioritization matrix is a tool that helps you focus on the most important items out of a set of choices. It allows you to identify the criteria you want to use to make your decision, and to assign relative weights to those criteria.

WHEN AND WHY IT'S USED IN WORKOUT

In the *Plan* phase, use a Prioritization Matrix:

- to select among potential WorkOut topics.

In the *Conduct* phase, use a Prioritization Matrix:

- to prioritize ideas.

WHAT TO DO

1. Identify criteria against which you will assess the items. Enter these on the matrix (See **Tool 17a** for an example that assesses four different ideas against the criteria of ROI, ease of implementation, and strategic impact).
2. Assign weights to indicate the relative importance of the different criteria. Enter these on the matrix.
3. Rate each item as high (9), medium (3), or low (1).
4. Multiply the rating for each criteria by the weight associated with that criteria.
5. Multiple the weights for all criteria for each item.
6. Look at absolute scores to determine relative priorities of the different choices.

SAMPLE PRIORITIZATION MATRIX

Ideas	ROI	Ease	Strategy	Absolute	Relative
			Criteria (High = 9, Med = 3, Low =1)		
				Priority	
Weight	*5*	*5*	*1*	—	—
Idea #1	9	1	1	225	4th
Idea #2	3	3	3	675	3rd
Idea #3	9	9	3	6075	1st
Idea #4	1	9	9	2025	2nd

Example: $(1 \times 5) \times (9 \times 5) \times (9 \times 1) = 2025$

Tool 17a.

NOTE:

In this Prioritization Matrix:

- *ROI:* size of the payoff for doing this
- *Ease:* how easy it is to implement
- *Strategy:* how connected this issue is to the organization's strategy

Idea #3 is the highest priority when assessed against these criteria, with these weights.

CHAPTER 18
Using Tools Related to the Analyze Phase of DMAIC

In this Chapter, we will address WorkOut-appropriate tools that are typically used in the Analyze phase of the DMAIC process:

1. The Five Whys
2. Cause-and-Effect Diagram
3. Flow Diagram

The Five Whys

WHAT IT IS

The Five Whys is a deceptively simple—but very effective—way of working toward the root cause of a problem or situation. It is so non-technical that it is a wonderful way to start all employees on the road to root-cause thinking.

WHEN AND WHY IT'S USED IN WORKOUT

In the *Conduct* phase, use the Five Whys:

- to help the Team discover underlying causes of the problems they have identified … and the causes of those causes.
- to ensure potential recommendations address causes rather than symptoms.
- to begin to establish and reinforce the discipline of root-cause thinking.

WHAT TO DO

1. Start with the focused problem statement.
2. Ask "why?" five times (See **Tool 18a**).

NOTE:

While the Five Whys is easy to use, it's very important that you do so in an atmosphere of non-threatening inquiry. This is particularly critical when you're using it with front-line workers. If workers feel that they are being asked to justify their actions, or defend themselves in any way, the Five Whys won't work. Instead, it may do more harm than good.

THE FIVE WHYS IN ACTION

Focused Problem Statement:

Customers complain about waiting too long to get connected
to staff during lunch hours.

Using the Five Whys:

WHY does this problem happen?

Backup operators take longer to connect callers.

→ **WHY** do backup operators take longer?

Backup operators don't know the job as well as the
regular operators/receptionists do.

→ **WHY** don't backup operators know the job as well?

There is no special training or job aid to make
up for the gap in experience and on-the-job
learning for the backups.

→ **WHY** isn't there special training or a job aid?

In the past, the organization has not
recognized this need.

→ **WHY** hasn't the organization recognized this
need? The organization has no system to
identify training needs.

Tool 18a.

Cause-and-Effect Diagram

WHAT IT IS

A Cause-and-Effect Diagram (also called a "fishbone diagram") graphically displays potential causes of a problem.
The purpose: to find the root cause(s).

It is common for people working on improvement efforts
to jump to conclusions without studying the causes, target
one possible cause while ignoring others, and take actions
aimed at surface symptoms. Cause-and-Effect Diagrams are
designed to guard against this.

The degree of root cause analysis required in WorkOut is
not as extensive as that used in Six Sigma, and typically does
not involve sophisticated statistical tools. The Cause-and-
Effect Diagram is at just the right level for WorkOut. It's effective enough, and is a good introduction to the root-cause
thinking required for a successful Six Sigma implementation.

WHEN AND WHY IT'S USED IN WORKOUT

In the *Conduct* phase, use Cause-and-Effect Diagrams:

- to organize ideas generated by brainstorming.
- to help the Team identify all potential causes of a problem … and the causes of those causes.
- to ensure potential recommendations address causes
  rather than symptoms.
- to begin to establish and reinforce the discipline of root-
  cause thinking.
- to help the Team communicate with others about the
  WorkOut process.

CAUSE-AND-EFFECT DIAGRAM

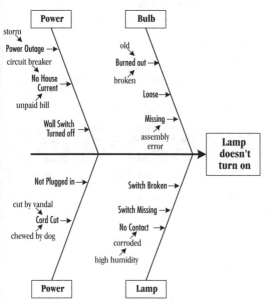

Tool 18b.

WHAT TO DO

1. Review the focused "problem statement."
2. Identify possible causes.
3. Sort possible causes into reasonable clusters.
4. Choose a cluster and label a main "bone."

5. Develop and arrange bones for that cluster.
6. Develop other main bones.
7. Select possible causes to verify with available data.

Flow Diagram

WHAT IT IS

A Flow Diagram is a graphical display that makes a process visible. There are three different types, each with its own purpose: (See **Tools 18c**, **18d**, and **18e**.)

Basic Flow Diagram	Activity Flow Diagram	Deployment Flow Diagram
To identify major steps of the process and where it begins and ends	To display complexity and decision points of the process	To help highlight handoff areas in process between people or functions
To illustrate where in the process you will collect data	To identify rework loops and bottlenecks	To clarify roles and indicate dependencies

WHEN AND WHY IT'S USED IN WORKOUT

In the *Plan* phase, use a Flow Diagram:

- to ensure agreement on the process to be examined.
- to include in the data pack for event participants.
- to identify what other data to collect.

In the *Conduct* phase, use a Flow Diagram:

- to create a common understanding of what's going on and who is doing what.
- to clarify the steps of the process.
- to uncover process problems and identify improvement opportunities such as complexity, handoffs, bottlenecks, delays, etc.
- to illustrate an alternative, streamlined process.

In the *Implement* phase, use a Flow Diagram:

- to train on the new process.
- to determine where to collect data for tracking the new process.

WHAT TO DO

(Hint: work with a group to get multiple viewpoints.)

1. Brainstorm action steps.
   - Write on sticky notes or a flipchart.
   - Make sure you include the steps that occur when things go wrong.
2. Arrange steps in sequence.
   - Be consistent in the direction of flow—time should flow top to bottom or left to right.
   - Use appropriate flow chart symbols.
3. Check for missing steps or decision points.
4. Number the steps.
5. Categorize steps as value-added or non-value-added. See **Tool 18f**.

NOTE:

> Be careful of your language here. Nobody wants to think
> that their job has no value. If you imply that this is the
> case, you can cause people to become defensive and
> unwilling to cooperate.

BASIC FLOW DIAGRAM

Tool 18c.

ACTIVITY FLOW DIAGRAM

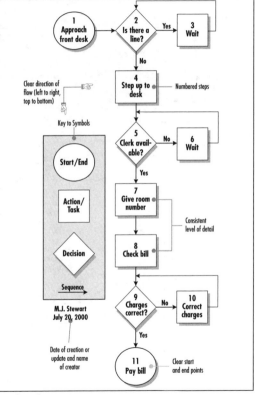

Tool 18d.

Deployment Flow Diagram, Invoicing Process

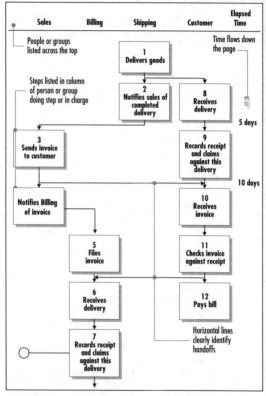

Tool 18e.

VALUE-ADDED VS. NON-VALUE-ADDED PROCESS STEPS

Characteristics of a Value-Added Step

☑ Customers are willing to pay for it.

☑ It physically changes the product.

☑ It's done right the first time.

Characteristics of a Non-Value-Added Step

☒ Not essential to product outcome.

☒ Does not add value to the output.

☒ Includes:

- defects, errors, omissions
- preparation/set-up, control/inspection
- over-production, processing, inventory
- transportation, motion, waiting, delays

Tool 18f.

CHAPTER 19
Using Tools Related to the Improve Phase of DMAIC

In this Chapter, we will address WorkOut-appropriate tools that are typically used in the Improve phase of the DMAIC process. We'll focus here on three creative techniques and one technique for managing risk:

1. Brainstorming
2. Twenty Questions
3. SCAMPER
4. FMEA

Brainstorming

WHAT IT IS

Brainstorming is a technique used to generate a lot of ideas quickly. It encourages creativity, involves everyone, generates excitement and energy, and separates people from the ideas they generate. The focus in Brainstorming is quantity, rather than quality.

WHEN AND WHY IT'S USED IN WORKOUT

In the *Plan* phase, use Brainstorming:

- to generate ideas for WorkOut topics and goals.

In the *Conduct* phase, use Brainstorming:

- to generate ideas for root causes of problems.
- to generate potential improvements to the process.
- to generate a list of things that might go wrong in the implementation of the improvements.

WHAT TO DO

1. Identify the Brainstorming method you'll use (see **Tool 19a**).
2. Follow the specific instructions for that method.
3. Start with silent "think" time. Remember, not everyone is comfortable with immediately speaking his/her thoughts, so give people time to consider what they'll say.
4. Freewheel—don't hold back.
5. No criticism or evaluation of ideas.
6. Hitchhike—build upon ideas.
7. The more ideas, the better.
8. Post ideas so everyone can see what's been said—this can help trigger more new ideas.

BRAINSTORMING FOR EVERYONE

Traditional Brainstorming
Appropriate when:
- Group members feel comfortable (in general) with speaking their thoughts aloud, quickly.
- Group members feel comfortable specifically with others in the group. Nobody feels too intimidated to join in.
- You're certain that no one member will dominate (this is less of an issue with "Rounds").

How it works:
- *Popcorn:* Anyone calls out ideas, no order, until all ideas are out.
- *Rounds:* Go around in turn, one item per person per turn, until everyone passes.

"Brainwriting"
Appropriate when:
- Some or all group members prefer to think before speaking and/or prefer writing to speaking.
- The group is mixed (seniority level, introverts/extroverts) and some members may feel somewhat intimidated.
- You suspect one or more members may dominate.

Tool 19a. (Continued on next page)

- *6-3-5 Method:*
  - Group of six people work together.
  - Each person writes down three ideas.
  - Pass idea papers clockwise to next person.
  - Person adds new ideas to this paper.
  - Repeat for a total of five rounds.
- *Brainwriting Pool Method:*
  - Group of five to eight people work together.
  - Each person writes down ideas in silence.
  - When out of ideas, place sheet in center of table and take another person's sheet.
  - Add new ideas to this sheet.
  - Continue for 20-30 minutes.

Tool 19a. (Continued)

Twenty Questions

WHAT IT IS

A structured series of questions that help a group generate improvement ideas.

WHEN AND WHY IT'S USED IN WORKOUT

In the *Conduct* phase, use Twenty Questions:

- to generate potential improvements to the process.

WHAT TO DO

For each step in the process you're improving, ask the questions listed in **Tool 19b**.

TWENTY QUESTIONS

What?	1. What happens now?
	2. Why do it?
	3. Can we do something else?
Who?	4. Who does it?
	5. Why them?
	6. Can someone else do it?
Where?	7. Where is it done?
	8. Why there?
	9. Can we do it elsewhere?
When?	10. When is it done?
	11. Why then?
	12. Can we do it some other time?
How?	13. How is it done?
	14. Why this way?
	15. Can we do it some other way?
For new processes	16. What should we do?
	17. Who should do it?
	18. Where should it be done?
	19. When should it be done?
	20. How should it be done?

Tool 19b.

SCAMPER

WHAT IT IS

A checklist that helps a group generate improvement ideas.
SCAMPER is a mnemonic for the items in the checklist.

WHEN AND WHY IT'S USED IN WORKOUT

In the *Conduct* phase, use SCAMPER:

• to generate potential improvements to the process.

WHAT TO DO

Work through the checklist in **Tool 19c** for each step of the
process. See what new ideas emerge.

SCAMPER

❏ Substitute	Can we think of a substitute for a process step, actor, input, or output?
❏ Combine	Can we combine this step with another one?
❏ Adapt	Can we adapt this step of the process in some way to get better results?
❏ Magnify	Can we do more of something to improve results?
❏ Put to Other Use	Can we put an input, actor, or output to some other use to improve results?
❏ Eliminate or Minimize	Can we eliminate a step, input, actor, or output, or do less of something, and get the same or better results?
❏ Reverse or Rearrange	Can we do things in the opposite or different order and get better results?

Tool 19c.

FMEA

What It Is

FMEA—which stands for *Failure Mode and Effect Analysis*—is a tool for predicting and managing risk. It helps you to identify what might go wrong, and what you might do if that happens.

When and Why It's Used in WorkOut

In the *Conduct* phase, use FMEA:

- to identify what might go wrong in the process of implementing improvement recommendations.
- to communicate with the Sponsor about your plan for dealing with risk (see description of Town Meeting in **Chapter 3** of this *Guide*).

What to Do

1. Use **Tool 19d**.
2. List the improvement ideas down the left side of the chart.
3. Brainstorm what might go wrong—these are the "failure modes."
4. Identify the effects of each failure, and rate its severity (you can use **Tool 19e** as a guideline).
5. Identify the specific actions you will take to reduce or eliminate the risk of each failure.

Note:

This is an abbreviated/simplified version of a FMEA.

FMEA Template

Idea	Potential Failure	Effect of Failure	Severity of Failure	Plan for Reducing/ Eliminating Risk
Idea # 1				
Idea # 2				
Idea # 3				
Idea # 4				

Tool 19d.

SAMPLE SEVERITY RATING SCALE

	Rating	Criteria: A failure could ...
bad	10	Injure a customer or employee
	9	Be illegal
	8	Render the product/service unfit for use
	7	Cause extreme customer dissatisfaction
	6	Result in partial malfunction
	5	Cause a loss of performance likely to result in a complaint
	4	Cause minor performance loss
	3	Cause a minor nuisance; can overcome with no loss
	2	Be unnoticed; minor effect on performance
good	1	Be unnoticed; no effect on performance

Tool 19e.

CHAPTER 20
Tools Related to the Control Phase of DMAIC

In this Chapter, we will address WorkOut-appropriate tools that are typically used in the Control phase of the DMAIC process:

1. Standardization
2. Evaluating Results

Standardization

WHAT IT IS

Standardization is making sure that important elements of a process are performed consistently in the best possible way. Changes are made only when the data shows that a new alternative is better.

WHEN AND WHY IT'S USED IN WORKOUT

In the *Implement* phase, use Standardization:

- as a means to capture and retain knowledge.
- to reduce variation among individuals and groups as they work on the process.
- to provide "know-why" for people now on the job.
- to provide a basis for training new people.
- to provide a trail for tracing problems.
- to give direction in the case of unusual conditions.

WHAT TO DO

See **Tool 20a** for guidance.

CREATING STANDARD PRACTICES AND PROCEDURES

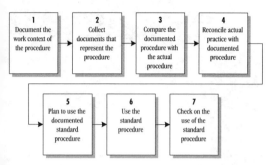

1	2	3	4
Document the work context of the procedure	Collect documents that represent the procedure	Compare the documented procedure with the actual procedure	Reconcile actual practice with documented procedure

5	6	7
Plan to use the documented standard procedure	Use the standard procedure	Check on the use of the standard procedure

Tool 20a.

Evaluating Results

WHAT IT IS

A quick method for looking at the results you got from a planned improvement and determining what to do next.

WHEN AND WHY IT'S USED IN WORKOUT

In the *Implement* phase, use Evaluating Results:

- to follow up on planned improvements.

WHAT TO DO

1. Using **Tool 20b**, identify where you fit on the matrix.
2. Follow the directions in the quadrant that describes your situation.

EVALUATING RESULTS

		Did you get acceptable results?	
		YES	**NO**
Did you follow your plan?	**YES**	You did what you planned to do and got the results you wanted. Move to hand-off.	You did what you planned to do, but did not get the results you wanted. Return to looking at causes, or perhaps the current situation. Study the gap. Get more data.
	NO	You got the results you wanted despite not doing what you planned to do. Determine the cause of the results—what did you unintentionally do right? Understand how to achieve good results, then move to hand-off.	You didn't do what you planned to do and you did not get the results you wanted. Return to your original plans. Would they have solved the problems you encountered? Try again with initial plans or revise as necessary.

Tool 20b.

PART 6

CHANGE MANAGEMENT AND FACILITATION TIPS FOR A SUCCESSFUL WORKOUT

This will come as no surprise to anyone who has actually done a Six Sigma project or a WorkOut: having technical know-how does not guarantee success.

To increase your chances of creating sustainable improvements, you should know how to:

• Get buy-in and cooperation from others.
• Manage a team.
• Facilitate an event.
• Communicate properly.

It is not the intent of this *Pocket Guide* to go into great detail on these topics. Instead, we will provide some basic "change management" and facilitation tips that can help you successfully use WorkOut for Six Sigma.

This Part gives you tools to:

1. Get buy-in and cooperation at the different phases of WorkOut.
2. Help you facilitate the WorkOut event.

See *Rath & Strong's Six Sigma Team Pocket Guide* for more on how to get buy-in/cooperation.

CHAPTER 21
Tips on Getting Buy-In and Cooperation at Each Phase of WorkOut

In this chapter, we will look at a couple of the key challenges at each phase of WorkOut, and offer tips on how to get the buy-in and cooperation you need to make WorkOut a success.

General Approach to Getting Buy-In and Cooperation

If you want people to give you their support and cooperation you can't just leave it to chance. The key is to think ahead about what you need, and from whom … and then create a plan to get it.

We call this approach *stakeholder management*, and it consists of three steps:

1. Stakeholder identification
2. Stakeholder analysis
3. Stakeholder planning

In **Chapter 16** of this book, we introduce stakeholder identification and a very basic version of stakeholder analysis. Here we will describe a more thorough version. Further, we will identify, for each WorkOut phase, the particular people and situations that may warrant stakeholder management.

NOTE:
> We assume here that you are the person organizing—or at least helping organize—the WorkOut. These suggested

actions are appropriate for the person pulling everything
together, or his/her advisor.

What to Do

1. Review **Tool 21a**. Are any of these relevant to your own
   WorkOut situation? Identify which ones you may want to
   consider for stakeholder management.
2. Refer back to **Chapter 16**, **Tool 16c**, and read through
   the list of stakeholders. Does this make you think of any
   additional stakeholder management "targets"? If so, add
   to your list from Step 1, above.
3. Use **Tool 21b** as a guideline for getting a thorough
   understanding of your target stakeholders.
4. Use **Tool 21c** as a guideline for putting together a plan
   to get buy-in, support, and cooperation from your target
   stakeholder(s).

Target Players/Situations for Stakeholder Management

Tool 21a lists potential targets by the WorkOut phase in
which you'd typically encounter them. Which ones will you
address?

WORKOUT PLAYERS AND SITUATIONS THAT MAY WARRANT STAKEHOLDER MANAGEMENT

Plan Phase

❑ Getting the **Team Leader**, **Sponsor**, and perhaps **others**, to *agree on a topic and goal* for the WorkOut.

❑ Ensuring the **Sponsor** is *sincere about involving front-line workers* in the WorkOut process, fully *understands the implications*, and will *have a bias toward accepting* reasonable recommendations from the Team.

❑ Ensuring that the **Sponsor** recognizes the need to *make a decision* at the WorkOut, and is prepared to do so.

Conduct Phase

❑ Getting the **Team Members** to not resist the WorkOut process, but to *participate fully* by contributing their knowledge about the details of the process, engaging in an exploration of the problem, helping identify and develop improvement ideas, etc.

❑ Getting **all participants**—Leaders, Members, Facilitators —to *follow the WorkOut process* and not disengage or let disagreements derail the process.

❑ Ensuring the **Sponsor** *fulfills his/her role* of challenging the Team, asking for opinions, taking risk, making clear decisions, etc. during the Town Meeting.

Tool 21a. (Continued on next page)

Implement Phase

❏ Ensuring that the **Sponsor** *follows through*: does not rescind any decisions, continues to support the WorkOut recommendations, provides needed guidance/assistance.

❏ Ensuring the **Team Leader** and **Team Members** continue to *follow the process* and *devote the necessary time, attention, and resources* to implementing and tracking the recommendations.

❏ Getting the **Team** and **financial expert** to *come to an agreement on the payoff* and how it is to be tracked.

Tool 21a. (Continued)

Stakeholder Analysis

Tool 21b provides a way for you to analyze your stakeholders—i.e., the people you've identified either through **Tool 21a** or **Tool 16c**.

STAKEHOLDER ANALYSIS WORKSHEET

Name of stakeholder/group:	
What I need from this stakeholder:	
Stakeholder's interests:	
How stakeholder may benefit from situation:	
How stakeholder may be hurt/ inconvenienced:	
Probable response from stakeholder. If resistance, why?	
How big a gap between what I need and probable response?	
Key influence "levers":	
Stakeholder's communication needs:	
Details/history of any conflict with stakeholder:	
Other relevant information about this stakeholder or situation:	

Tool 21b.

EXPLANATION OF WORKSHEET ELEMENTS

What I need from this stakeholder: Behaviors listed in **Tool 21a**—resources, information, permission, time, etc.

Stakeholder's Interests: These are tangible and intangible, such as desire to keep job, money, resources, need to be seen as competent, power, reputation, sense of fairness, etc.

How stakeholder may benefit: What person might perceive as a potential gain from the outcome/activities relating to this situation, or interests that could be satisfied.

How stakeholder might be hurt or inconvenienced: What person might perceive as a loss or unpleasant result from the outcome/activities relating to this situation … or interests that could be imperiled.

Probable response from stakeholder: Whether you think person will be supportive, resistant, or neutral. What you think person might actually do.

Size of gap for this stakeholder: Gap between person's probable response and what you need. (This helps you prioritize your stakeholder planning activities.)

Key influence "levers": Key items that will help you influence this person, such as his/her interests that you can help address, shared values that will help smooth the way, etc.

Stakeholder's communication needs: Person's preferred way of communicating (in person vs. phone vs. e-mail; words vs. pictures; detail vs. summary, etc.)

Details/history of conflict with stakeholder: Any past or anticipated conflict with this person; any area in which what you're asking of this person may come into conflict with his/her goal or organizational role.

Other relevant information about stakeholder: e.g., Who are his/her allies, and do you have a relationship with any of them?

Stakeholder Planning

Tool 21c provides a way for you to plan for getting support and cooperation from the stakeholders you've identified and just finished analyzing.

STAKEHOLDER PLANNING WORKSHEET

Name of stakeholder/group:	
Specific influence objective:	
How to increase (or reframe) benefits to this stakeholder:	
How to reduce (or reframe) "cost" or inconvenience to this stakeholder:	
How to deal with any current or anticipated conflict with this stakeholder:	
Plan for direct influence:	
Plan for indirect influence:	
Implementation considerations (including timing and communications approach):	

Tool 21c.

EXPLANATION OF WORKSHEET ELEMENTS

Specific influence objective: Describe in detail exactly what you want the person to do, and what will happen if you are successful in influencing him/her (i.e., what will it look like?).

How to increase benefits: Identify anything you—or someone with whom you have influence—can do to ensure that person benefits from the outcome/activities relating to this situation. Think of how you might change person's perception if you see a benefit and he/she does not. If person already sees a benefit, consider how you can reinforce that perception.

How to reduce cost/inconvenience: Identify anything you—or someone with whom you have influence—can do to reduce the negative effects of the outcome/activities on person. Think of how you might change person's perception if he/she sees a cost/inconvenience but you do not believe it will happen.

How to deal with conflict: Write down your thoughts about a good approach to resolving the conflict, given what (if anything) you know about yourself and the person's conflict style.

Plan for direct influence: Identify your strategy for influencing this person, and how you will communicate with him/her in the course of so doing.

Plan for indirect influence: If you are not the best one to influence person directly, think about whom you could ask to do it for you. Consider whether you have access to any materials, information or meetings, or contact with industry peers, etc., that might help. If your stakeholder is a group, try to identify a friend or contact in that group who might serve as an informal link.

Implementation considerations: Identify the steps you'll take, when you'll take them, and whether anything else has to happen first. Determine communication methods and content.

CHAPTER 22
Tips on Facilitating the WorkOut Event

Facilitation

As we'll refer to it in this *Guide*, facilitation is the ability to contribute to a WorkOut Team's effectiveness by simultaneously:

- guiding the team through the structured WorkOut process, ensuring that it stays on track.
- paying attention to the "team dynamics" in the group, and taking steps to maintain effective interactions between team members during the *Conduct* and *Implement* phases.

Role of the Facilitator in the WorkOut Phases

Typically, the WorkOut Designer (as described in **Chapter 2** of this *Guide*) also acts as the lead Facilitator for the entire WorkOut event. So you'll see these terms used interchangeably.

The role of the Facilitator varies during the different phases of WorkOut:

Plan	Conduct	Implement
Prepare the WorkOut.	Guide Teams through the WorkOut process. Keep Teams on track. Manage Team dynamics. Help Team develop Town Meeting presentation.	Work with Team Leader to ensure Team stays focused. Manage Team dynamics.

Key Facilitation Competencies

Effective facilitation requires two critical competencies, both of which come into play in WorkOut:

Recognition: The ability to perceive (or make a diagnosis about) what is going on during a Team Meeting and recognize problems or obstacles to effective performance.

Intervention: The ability to take appropriate action based on a diagnosis, and to provide the team with appropriate structure, guidance, tools, and insights.

Difficult Situations

Experienced Facilitators can tell stories about nightmare meetings, where nothing seemed to go right no matter how hard they tried. Even the most seasoned Facilitators can be challenged by difficult Team situations. Don't let this happen to you in WorkOut!

What to Do

1. Anticipate Team problems—don't be surprised.
2. View disruptive behavior as a group, rather than an individual, problem.
3. Use **Tool 22a** as your first guide for recognizing and intervening in a difficult situation.
4. Use **Tool 22b** for some hints on dealing with brief disruptions.
5. Use **Tool 22c** for more detailed suggestions on how to handle tough situations.

GOALS, ROLES, AND PROCEDURES PYRAMID AND GUIDELINES

Problem Area	Where to Look for Possible Causes
Interpersonal Relationships: Team members don't get along, are in conflict, argue.	Start a level up, at Procedures • Are the right team procedures in place? • Have members agreed to them? • Are they being enforced? If Procedures OK, move up again to Roles: • Are team member roles clearly defined? • Do members agree to their roles? Are roles free from conflict? If Roles OK, move up again to Goals • Are team goals clear? • Do members agree to the goals? • Are goals free of conflict?

Tool 22a. (Continued on next page)

Tips on Facilitating the WorkOut Event

Problem Area	Where to Look for Possible Causes
Procedures: Members don't follow procedures, or argue about them, or don't seem to know what they are.	Start up a level, at *Roles*: • Are Team member roles clearly defined? • Do members agree to their roles? • Are roles free from conflict? If *Roles* OK, move up again to *Goals*: • Are Team goals clear? • Do members agree to the goals?
Roles: Members don't fulfil the responsibilities of their roles, argue about them, don't seem to know what they are.	Start up a level, at *Goals*: • Are Team goals clear? • Do members agree to the goals? • Are goals free of conflict?

Tool 22a. (Continued)
Reference: Rubin, Plovnick, and Fry, *Task-Oriented Project Development*

GENERAL INTERVENTION MODEL

Start with the least confrontational approach

Ignore or avoid

Make eye contact

Stand up

Walk halfway to individual

Engage individual in discussion

Allude to disruptive behavior and redirect in positive direction

Speak to individual on a break

Speak to individual in the meeting and involve Team

Tool 22b.

DEALING WITH DIFFICULT TEAM SITUATIONS

The Silent Group: *Not a peep out of them!*

Why?	Do's	Don'ts
• Group is new • No interest in topic • Feel outcome is preordained • Environment feels unsafe • Lack of understanding • Confused • Unprepared • Fear of failure • Don't want to be there • Intimidated by others	☑ Call on people ☑ Break Team into smaller groups ☑ Go around table for ideas ☑ Introduce challenge or fun activity	✗ Emphasize that group is quiet or not participating ✗ Be wildly energetic yourself

The Silent Participant: *Nothing to say?*

Why?	Do's	Don'ts
• Reluctant to speak in group: shy, intimidated, needs time to form thoughts, etc. • Confused • Lost • Bored • Disinterested • Negative	☑ Use open-ended questions ☑ Use nominal group technique ☑ Acknowledge contributions ☑ Control members who dominate	✗ Call on person unless you know he/she has something to share

Tool 22c. (Continued on next page)

Tips on Facilitating the WorkOut Event

The Dominator: *Seems like the only person in the room*

Why?	Do's	Don'ts
• Strong personality • Very extroverted • Need for limelight • Passion about the issue • High level of expertise • Own agenda • High need for control • Misunderstanding of process • Nervousness	☑ Ask others for reaction ☑ Use small groups or nominal group technique ☑ Avoid eye contact with individual ☑ Restate & focus on goal	× Compete with or attack person

The Interfering Sponsor: *Full of helpful (or not) ideas*

Why?	Do's	Don'ts
• Habit of being in charge • Fear of losing power or control • Fear of being made to look bad at the Town Meeting	☑ Acknowledge input and move on ☑ Tactfully ask individual to leave ☑ Reference ground rules ☑ Suggest non-meeting responsibility ☑ Ask for input outside the meeting	× Criticize

Tool 22c. (Continued on next page)

Tips on Facilitating the WorkOut Event

The Raging Bull: *What's he/she so angry about?*

Why?	Do's	Don'ts
• Long-standing frustration • Unrelated conflict with another Team member(s) • Feeling attacked • Feeling contributions are not heard	☑ Use conflict management tools ☑ Emphasize common goals ☑ Address root cause of anger ☑ Use humor to lighten the mood ☑ Take a break	✗ React with anger or defensiveness ✗ Take sides ✗ Force the group to move on if there's a serious disagreement

The Pain in the Neck: *Everything is a production!*

Why?	Do's	Don'ts
• Disagreement over the topic or process • Forced participation • Unrelated problems	☑ Talk about how it makes you feel ☑ Refer to agenda ☑ Offer a productive task or activity	✗ Assume you know motives ✗ Compete ✗ Insult or embarrass

The Rambler: *Does this person ever take a breath?*

Why?	Do's	Don'ts
• Lack of clarity or knowledge about the issue under discussion • Discomfort discussing the issue	☑ Provide structure ☑ Interrupt ☑ Summarize comments concisely and move on task or activity	✗ Cut speaker off or move on before you can summarize the point and get person's agreement

Tool 22c. (Continued on next page)

191

The Savior: *What would we do without him/her?*		
Why?	**Do's**	**Don'ts**
• Has solution in mind and is determined to get group to accept it	☑ Acknowledge contribution ☑ Capture idea on flipchart ☑ Identify related issues ☑ Resist premature decision-making	✕ Dismiss the solution ✕ Appear not to listen

The Participating Facilitator: *Unclear on own role*		
Why?	**Do's**	**Don'ts**
• Gets sucked into the content of the conversation	☑ Focus on accurate scribing ☑ Allow a 6-second pause before speaking ☑ Ask someone else to facilitate briefly ☑ Acknowledge slip and step back into role	✕ Continue to put forth your view

Tool 22c. (Continued)

CONCLUSION

As consultants, we find that it's often risky to tell leaders and managers that a particular approach "worked for General Electric."

Knowing that GE did something does indeed makes some clients more receptive to an idea. But we wish we had a dollar for every person who immediately pointed out that—in case we hadn't noticed—they were not working at GE.

Both groups can be on solid ground. "Stealing" great ideas from a successful company can be good business practice—but only if the idea is appropriate for your organization. If it is, you can get better results with less time, money, and grief. The trick is to distinguish ideas that are great and appropriate from those that are neither.

If your organization is involved in Six Sigma, and you're wondering whether WorkOut is worthwhile, here's our advice: *steal this idea*. At the very least, don't dismiss it without a try.

We started this book with a bold statement:

No matter where you are with Six Sigma—getting ready to roll it out, experiencing difficulties with an existing initiative, or implementing it successfully—WorkOut has a role to play.

We hope we've succeeded at backing this up with a clear explanation, useful examples, and some practical guidance.

Good luck!

APPENDIX A
Six Examples of "WorkOut for Six Sigma" Topics and Goals, and Why They Work

Using WorkOut to *Prepare* for Six Sigma, Example 1

Topic: Streamline the monthly invoicing process in Billing Department.

Goal: Reduce the elapsed time between month end and the mailing of invoices from current 10 business days to three by the end of this quarter.

Why It Works: Targets highly visible process that has been a source of concern in Sales and a top priority for new COO, who will publicize results.

Frees up resources from non-value-added work and makes them available to partner with line on revenue-producing tasks (and, eventually, on financial part of Six Sigma).

Gives billing clerks a way to get their improvement ideas put into effect, building worker empowerment.

Can get results quickly, with minimum of data collection, so will be good example of how process improvement can work in administrative functions.

Using WorkOut to *Prepare* for Six Sigma, Example 2

Topic: Improve customer service in the package delivery process.

Goal: Increase on-time delivery of special-billing packages from current level of 50% to 90%, thus reducing refunds paid by 80%, in the next 90 days.

Why It Works: Shows how proactively fixing a process problem can be more effective than a fire-fighting approach that depends on heroic efforts to meet customer demands.

Shows how an approach that involves participation of front-line workers can be successful.

Provides opportunity to introduce front-line workers to basic Six Sigma tools to in the context of improving their own performance:

- VOC
- SIPOC/Flow Diagram
- Five Whys
- Cause-and-Effect Diagram

Will create energy for additional process improvement work.

Using WorkOut to *Reenergize* Your Six Sigma Initiative, Example 1

Topic: Improve mortgage application process.

Goal: Reduce the percentage of mortgage applications that must be returned to applicants for additional information by 50% by end of January.

Why It Works: Frees up six people who are doing this (re)work and allows them to help with data collection on department's Six Sigma projects.

Empowers front-line workers to work on eliminating tasks they all dislike.

Likely to be accomplished earlier than deadline—fast results possible.

Using WorkOut to *Reenergize* Your Six Sigma Initiative, Example 2

Topic: Improve collections process.

Goal: Reduce collections backlog by 50%, which represents $21M, by end of quarter.

Why It Works: Potential for big payoff in short period of time. Will keep division energized and willing to continue more complex and time-consuming process improvement efforts.

Big payoff will also allow Directors to recognize savings during current financial period, positively affecting their quarterly bonuses.

Will give Directors more positive impression of process improvement effort and what it can do for them, thus making them more inclined to cooperate and assign resources to Six Sigma projects.

Using WorkOut to *Complement* and *Enhance* Your Six Sigma Initiative, Example 1

Topic: Improve Call Center customer service.

Goal: Reduce percent of calls that require supervisor handling by 50% over next two months.

Why It Works: Topic of major concern to Call Center Director, who is trying to do more with less. Director has been lobbying for months to make this a Six Sigma project, which it is not, and will welcome any help in solving this issue.

Good proof-of-concept for WorkOut—will reduce pressure from Directors to make everything a Six Sigma project.

Frees up resources (supervisors) to assist with any of the four ongoing Six Sigma projects in the Call Center.

Using WorkOut to *Complement* and *Enhance* Your Six Sigma Initiative, Example 2

Topic: Project Team has encountered Gage R&R problem in Measure phase of project addressing variation in auto tank blow-molding process.

Goal: Using WorkOut, fix system for measuring tank volume so that by end of month, measurements are repeatable and reproducible and DMAIC project can continue.

Why It Works: Enhances DMAIC process by incorporating WorkOut approach.

Involves front-line workers who are experienced with the current measurement system.

- Gives Six Sigma project team the benefit of workers' extensive knowledge of system.
- Allows workers to participate in visible project in a way that can build their buy-in for the project goal and the overall DMAIC approach.

APPENDIX B
But What About Lean Six Sigma?

By now you've seen how WorkOut can help you prepare for, reenergize, complement or enhance your Six Sigma initiative.

But maybe you're wondering ... can WorkOut also play a role in Lean Six Sigma?

A very good question. And the answer is ... YES! (Why else would we have this Appendix?)

While this *Pocket Guide* focuses on Six Sigma, a somewhat similar approach can be used within a Lean Six Sigma initiative. The purpose of this Appendix is to briefly address this topic.

But before we get into any specifics, let's quickly clarify how we're using the term "Lean Six Sigma."

Lean Six Sigma

We use "Lean Six Sigma" to describe an approach that involves using the principles, methods, and tools of both Six Sigma and Lean to improve process performance.

We use DMAIC as an overarching problem-solving technique to help us determine specifically what is needed to improve a particular process, and then to ensure that we do the things that work.

At a very high level, the approach can be described as shown in **Tool B1**.

THE LEAN SIX SIGMA APPROACH

Define	• Set project goals and boundaries based on the needs of the business, the customer, and the process. • Select and begin defining the project value stream.
Measure	• Build a factual understanding of existing process conditions and establish a capability level baseline. • Complete a current state Value Stream Map to establish a process baseline for the value stream.
Analyze	• Develop theories of root causes, confirm theories with data, and identify the root cause(s). • Analyze the value stream to design a future state with the shortest lead time, highest quality, and lowest cost possible.
Improve	• Develop, implement, and evaluate solutions targeted at the verified root cause(s). • Design, implement, and debug a cell with the shortest lead time, highest quality, and lowest cost possible.
Control	• Ensure that the new value stream meets/exceeds goals, that the problem stays solved, and that the new methods can be further improved.

Tool B1.

How Does WorkOut Fit with Lean Six Sigma?

We can describe the role of WorkOut for Lean Six Sigma with the same organizing framework that we used throughout this *Pocket Guide*. We'll briefly address how WorkOut can help you prepare for, reenergize, complement, and enhance a Lean Six Sigma initiative.

Preparing for Lean Six Sigma

The "readiness" factors that are required for Six Sigma are also required for Lean Six Sigma. The common problems (and causes) are also present.

Some factors, however, take on a larger role when Lean is added to the mix. The effect on front-line workers is broader, more immediate, more obvious, and (potentially) more profound. So the readiness factors that involve these workers take on greater significance.

Specifically, these factors warrant extra attention in a Lean Six Sigma initiative: (refer to **Tool 5b** for a fuller description).

1. An organizational culture that is participative rather than hierarchical.
2. An organizational culture that values prevention and the development of good processes over "fire-fighting," and that doesn't reward "heroics."

The *participation vs. hierarchy* factor should be clear: Lean requires the total involvement and cooperation of front-line workers from the very start of the initiative. While these employees should, of course, be involved in Six Sigma projects, their participation will likely be earlier and more intense when Lean is involved.

If management does not have a history of involving these workers, or is not inclined to do so, it is going to be very difficult for the organization to implement Lean Six Sigma successfully.

The *prevention vs. fire-fighting* factor is perhaps less obvious. The thinking here is that making processes "Lean" takes away many of the issues that lead to the need for fire-fighting and other types of organizational "heroics."

Are your front-line workers and their supervisors accustomed to getting recognition for heroic efforts (and maybe for nothing else!)? If so, it is going to be very difficult to get them to support the change to a situation in which those efforts are no longer needed.

In addition to increasing emphasis on these two existing factors, we also suggest that at least one more readiness factor comes into play when Lean is added to the mix. Specifically:

> *A broad group of stakeholders—from senior management to the front line—must be willing to abandon what may be deeply held beliefs about how processes work. They must be open to trying an approach that might seem counterintuitive and unworkable.*

Many of the principles and solutions of Lean require people to suspend their belief and try something completely different. See **Tool B2**.

ABANDONING DEEPLY HELD BELIEFS ON WHAT WORKS

These stakeholders	must accept that...
Senior Management	... efforts are better spent creating "pull" than perfecting a forecasting system.
Finance Directors	... it can be more cost-effective not to run machines at their maximum production rate, but rather to run them at takt time.
Managers	... having work-in-process inventory increases throughput time, and is therefore to be eliminated wherever possible, and not kept as a "cushion."
Supervisors	... reorganizing into cells and balancing the workload will result in greater efficiencies than any previous attempts they may have made.
Front-Line Workers	... working on various tasks at takt time can be more efficient than working on one task as quickly as possible

Tool B2.

GIVEN THE ABOVE, WHAT ROLE CAN WORKOUT PLAY?

WorkOut can help you prepare for a Lean Six Sigma initiative by addressing these readiness factors as follows:

Hierarchical vs. Participative Culture: WorkOut can help by pushing decisions down the hierarchy, empowering front-line workers. Further, it can show senior management the benefits of getting these workers involved in fixing processes.

Prevention vs. Fire-Fighting Culture: WorkOut can help by rewarding groups (through quick and confirming decisions) for solving process problems. It is also a quick way of introducing cause-and-effect thinking and a process perspective—both necessary for a successful Lean Six Sigma implementation.

Abandoning Deeply Held Beliefs of What Works: WorkOut's effect on this factor is indirect, and focused primarily on front-line workers. The participative nature of WorkOut can help build workers' trust in management. This can increase the chance that the workers will be willing to try a new idea…even if it seems counterintuitive.

Reenergizing a Lean Six Sigma Initiative

Initiatives need reenergizing when they show signs of trouble that go beyond the normal ups and downs. The signs of trouble in a Six Sigma initiative (see **Tool 9a**) also apply to Lean Six Sigma. We'd add to that list at least one additional sign:

> *Front-line workers and their supervisors refuse to participate in the improvement process.*

Potential underlying causes of this problem include some of those found in **Tool 9b**, and also:

- Worker fear of job loss (due to Lean's explicit goal of

doing the most work with the least resources)

- Supervisor fear of losing control or face (due to the impact Lean-related changes have on the day-to-day activities of the front-line workers)

GIVEN THE ABOVE, WHAT ROLE CAN WORKOUT PLAY?

WorkOut can address the above underlying causes indirectly, as a result of its participative nature. Specifically:

- It can help build trust, as workers see that management is willing to involve them in decisions about their work
- It can involve supervisors in a way that will mitigate their concerns about losing control or face

Complementing/Enhancing a Lean Six Sigma Initiative

In **Chapter 13** of this *Pocket Guide*, we described how you can *complement* an existing Six Sigma initiative by applying WorkOut to issues that Six Sigma doesn't address.

The situation with Lean Six Sigma is no different. Yes, Lean Six Sigma expands the scope of the initiative to include additional problem-solving techniques. But there will still be problems best solved through another approach. The method for screening problems for WorkOut (see **Tool 13b**) still applies.

In **Chapter 14,** we described how you can *enhance* an existing Six Sigma initiative by using WorkOut practices within the stages of DMAIC, and by using "behavioral habits" from WorkOut at all stages of projects.

Here, again, the situation with Lean Six Sigma is no different. As we defined it at the start of this chapter, Lean Six Sigma uses the DMAIC method as an overarching problem-solving approach. The use of WorkOut practices within each phase (see **Tool 14a**) is still appropriate.

Similarly, the behavioral habits of WorkOut—as described in **Tool 14b**—still apply. The need for the habits described in *Approach to Front-Line Workers and General Inclusiveness* may be even greater in initiatives that involve Lean than in those involving only Six Sigma.

• • •

In summary, WorkOut has a role to play whether your initiative is limited to Six Sigma or expanded to include Lean. In either case, it can help you prepare for, reenergize, or complement/enhance your initiative.

Further Reading

Rath & Strong's Six Sigma Pocket Guide (Rath & Strong, 2000)

Rath & Strong's Six Sigma Team Pocket Guide (McGraw-Hill, 2003)

Rath & Strong's Six Sigma Champion's Pocket Guide (Rath & Strong, 2003)

Rath & Strong's Six Sigma Leadership Handbook (Wiley, 2003)

Rath & Strong's Six Sigma Advanced Tools Pocket Guide (McGraw-Hill, 2004)

Rath & Strong's Six Sigma/DMAIC Road Map (Rath & Strong, 2002)

Rath & Strong's Lean Six Sigma Road Map (Rath & Strong, 2005)

The GE Work-Out: How to Implement GE's Revolutionary Method for Busting Bureaucracy and Attacking Organizational Problems—Fast! Dave Ulrich, Steve Kerr, and Ron Ashkenas (McGraw-Hill, 2002)